D1131075

LEGENDARY SPORTS WRITERS OF THE GOLDEN AGE

LEGENDARY SPORTS WRITERS OF THE GOLDEN AGE

Grantland Rice, Red Smith, Shirley Povich, and W. C. Heinz

Lee Congdon

ROWMAN & LITTLEFIELD
Lanham • Boulder • New York • London

Published by Rowman & Littlefield
A wholly owned subsidiary of The Rowman & Littlefield Publishing Group,
Inc.
4501 Forbes Boulevard, Suite 200, Lanham, Maryland 20706
www.rowman.com

Unit A, Whitacre Mews, 26-34 Stannary Street, London SE11 4AB

British Library Cataloguing in Publication Information Available

Library of Congress Cataloging-in-Publication Data

Names: Congdon, Lee, 1939– author.
Title: Legendary sports writers of the golden age : Grantland Rice, Red Smith, Shirley Povich, and
    W.C. Heinz / Lee Congdon.
Description: Lanham : Rowman & Littlefield, [2017] | Includes bibliographical references and
    index.
Identifiers: LCCN 2016043504 (print) | LCCN 2017005692 (ebook) | ISBN 9781442277519
    (cloth : alk. paper) | ISBN 9781442277526 (electronic)
Subjects: LCSH: Rice, Grantland, 1880–1954. | Smith, Red, 1905–1982. | Povich, Shirley. | Heinz,
    W. C. (Wilfred Charles), 1915–2008. | Sportswriters—United States—Biography. | Sports
    journalism—United States—History—20th century.
Classification: LCC GV742.4 .C66 2017 (print) | LCC GV742.4 (ebook) | DDC 796.0922 [B]—
    dc23 LC record available at https://lccn.loc.gov/2016043504

♾ ™ The paper used in this publication meets the minimum requirements of
American National Standard for Information Sciences Permanence of Paper
for Printed Library Materials, ANSI/NISO Z39.48-1992.

Printed in the United States of America

To Carol, Mitchell, Colleen, and Jennifer

CONTENTS

PREFACE

This is an appreciation of four writers who devoted their considerable talents to covering the world of sports. They did so for a variety of reasons, not the least of which was living and working during the Golden Age of Sports. When people speak of the Golden Age of Sports, they are generally referring to the 1920s—the time of Babe Ruth, Bobby Jones, Jack Dempsey, and Red Grange. The argument advanced here, however, is that the Golden Age continued on through the 1930s, 1940s, and, especially, 1950s, before coming to an end in about 1963. In the fall of that year, President Kennedy was assassinated, and almost at the same time, the historical (as opposed to the chronological) decade of the 1960s began. The United States and American sports would never be the same.

With the exception of Grantland Rice, my subjects—Red Smith, Shirley Povich, and W. C. Heinz—lived on into the new era, but their best work continued to concern athletes and events of the Golden Age, which was one of the reasons they constituted an informal fraternity. But there were others. They covered many of the same events, admired one another's work, and socialized when opportunity presented itself. When in Manhattan, these writers headed straight for Toots Shor's—the "Mother Lodge," as Red Smith called the famous saloon-restaurant—where they knew they would be joining athletes and members of their guild.

Like all good writers, each of them developed a distinctive style. Grantland Rice's celebration of great athletes reflected a poetic sensibility. Because of his command of the English language, Red Smith followed Rice in moving sports writing in a literary direction. Shirley Povich not only continued in the Rice–Smith tradition, but also displayed a rare sympathy for those athletes whom critics took to task for their failures both on and off the field. A novelist at heart, W. C. Heinz adopted a style similar to the one made famous by Ernest Hemingway, while striving to remind readers that athletes are human beings, not simply performers. Taken together, these four writers lifted sports reporting to heights that it is unlikely to reach again, which is why it is important to remember them and the remarkable era they immortalized.

I

THE POET

Grantland Rice

Americam sports writing, insofar as it counts as a literary pursuit, owes a lasting debt to Grantland Rice. Having earned a degree in classics from Vanderbilt University, Granny (as his friends called him) brought to his chosen profession broad learning and a conviction that great athletes were actors in a drama as heroic and meaningful as that of the ancient Greeks. Possessing a poetic nature, he found time, while publishing more than 67 million words as a journalist, to craft more than seven thousand verses, some of them of high quality; he regularly began a column with lines of verse.

Henry Grantland Rice was born in Murfreesboro, Tennessee, on November 1, 1880. The place was the scene of an important Civil War battle, fought on July 13, 1862. Led by General Nathan Bedford Forrest, the Confederate Army defeated Union forces and, in the process, established their leader's reputation. Rice's maternal grandfather, Henry Grantland, took part in the battle and spoke to his grandson of his admiration for Forrest and lack of respect for the more senior General Braxton Bragg. Although regarded as incompetent, even by his own men, Bragg treated Forrest as a mere raider who lacked the West Point education he himself possessed. Not a man to suffer fools gladly, Forrest once dressed Bragg down in words not customarily used in addressing a senior officer: "You have threatened to arrest me for not obeying your orders promptly. I dare you to do it, and I say to you that if you ever again try to interfere with me or cross my path, it will be at the peril of your life."

Forrest was, and continues to be, a controversial figure, in part because of his April 12, 1864, capture of Fort Pillow in Henning, Tennessee, during the course of which defenders, many of whom were black, were either killed after refusing to surrender or executed. After the war, he joined the Ku Klux Klan, although whether he was ever the Grand Wizard remains uncertain. Nevertheless, because of his courage, daring, and military gifts (without having had formal military training), Forrest was a hero to Tennessee boys, including Grantland Rice, who admired men of adventure and courage, and displayed it himself, when, already famous, 37 years of age, married, and the father of one, he, like Bedford Forrest in the Civil War, enlisted as a private when the United States entered World War I. "On thru whatever hells may wait," he wrote in a verse about the lure of battle for the *New York Times*, "With marching feet and rolling drum/Beyond the final grip of Fate/The Great Adventure whispers 'Come!'"

Due to his maturity and celebrity, Rice quickly rose to sergeant and then second lieutenant of the artillery. Originally assigned to work with the *Stars and Stripes*, the military newspaper, he sought and was assigned a role in the Meuse–Argonne Offensive (September 26–November 11, 1918), during which he faced real danger, although as an artilleryman he was stationed near the rear of the front. He survived but never forgot those who did not. In "A Marine Comes Home," he wrote of John W. Overton of Tennessee, killed in action in July 1918.

> He has come home again to find old dreams
> Beneath the shelter of his native sky,
> By friendly hills, lost lanes, and singing streams
> Where winds, blown out of morning, rustle by
> To whisper to him through the guarding pines
> That cast deep shadows down the silent glen,
> Or call to him through spring's new blossomed vines:
> "The guns are still—and you are home again."

On each anniversary of Armistice Day (November 11), he devoted his column to the memory of those who were killed.

The year of Rice's birth (1880) was as important to his future life as its place. He came of age before 1914, and that more innocent period in U.S. history remained, for him, the world as it ought to be. During those early years, he studied at Vanderbilt and played baseball and football, the latter being his favorite sport. Years later he explained why: "Because football calls for courage, both the highest physical and mental condition, because of its ruggedness, I suppose I like football more than any other sport."

Still, in time he came to love golf, both as a fan and a low-handicap player, as well as almost every other sport. Like anyone who has engaged in athletics at any level, he enjoyed winning, but near the end of his life he wrote in his memoirs that he always "learned a lot more from defeat than [he] ever learned from winning." From his earliest years, he believed the immortal lines he wrote in 1908, in a verse entitled "Alumnus Football": "For when the One Great Scorer comes to write against your name/He marks—not that you won or lost—but how you played the Game." Had he written nothing else, Rice would occupy a secure place in American culture.

These lines have been cited so often they qualify as a cliché, but that is only a result of their repetitive citing, and they are quoted often because they bear witness to a profound truth, even more so in times since Granny penned them, when winning at all costs is all that seems to matter—with the resulting damage to the characters of those who compete and those who cheer them on. At the time he wrote "Alumnus Football," Rice was working for the *Nashville Tennessean* (after stops at the *Atlanta Journal* and the *Cleveland News*), coaching the Vanderbilt baseball team, and refereeing football games for Vanderbilt, Sewanee (University of the South), and the University of Tennessee.

Obviously, he loved sports. But let him speak for himself in these lines from a verse he wrote in June 1907, shortly after beginning work at the *Tennessean*:

> I'd like to go to heaven and yet it brings me tears
> To think I'll never see a game through many million years—
> The six months rest from fall to spring seems awful long to me—
> So tell me then how I could last through an eternity?

Just as obviously, Rice loved the South and its culture, one of the charming representatives of which was his old friend, Joel Chandler Harris. For many years an editor at the *Atlanta Constitution*, Harris achieved fame for his wonderful "Uncle Remus" stories. Uncle Remus is a wise and kindly old black man who regales the young son of a plantation owner with folktales about "Brer Rabbit," "Brer Fox," and other animals. When Harris died in 1908, Rice composed a memorial verse entitled "Uncle Remus (Upon the Death of Joel Chandler Harris)." One of his moving quatrains reads:

> The Little Boy is lonesome and his eyes are filled with tears;
> Beyond the mists he only sees the shadows of the years;
> The light now lies behind him with his best friend gone away;
> But the softest winds in Dixie at his heart will kneel to pray.

Although in *his* heart he never left the South, Rice knew that to reach readers throughout the nation he had to pursue his career in New York. In early 1911, therefore, he accepted a position with the New York-based *Evening Mail*. The city was then home to the baseball Giants of John McGraw, a combative, profane, and hard-drinking Irishman with a taste, if not a knack, for gambling. He and Rice quickly became friends, although Granny preferred the company of the Giants' Christy Mathewson, one of the game's greatest pitchers. At a time when players were generally a coarse and unruly lot, many of them drunks and some illiterate, "Matty" stood out as a man of education (he studied for three years at Bucknell University) and good character.

During the span of his Hall of Fame career, Matty won 373 games (79 by shutout) and lost only 188. His lifetime ERA (earned run average) was 2.13. He started 551 games and completed 434 of them. In 4,780.2 innings pitched, he issued an almost unbelievably low number of bases on balls, at 844. In the 1905 World Series, against Connie Mack's Philadelphia Athletics, he performed a matchless feat of pitching, shutting out the A's three times in six days. Rice covered that Series for the *Atlanta Journal*, and from then on he regarded Mathewson as the "greatest pitcher [he] ever saw"; when he arrived in New York, he and Matty forged a close friendship.

As Rice's fame grew, he became increasingly dissatisfied with the money the *Evening Mail* was able to pay, and, on January 1, 1915, he jumped to the *New-York Tribune*, founded by Horace Greeley in 1841. In addition to greater prestige, the paper offered him syndication; by the time of his enlistment, his "Sportlight" column was appearing in more than 80 papers throughout the country. He had become the most famous and highest-paid sports writer in the United States.

When he arrived home from Europe in February 1919, Granny, like all those who had experienced war, was a changed man. He recognized with sadness that the "lightheartedness that the world knew" in the prewar years was forever lost, and he dreamed "of France and of those who made a crossing much bigger than those of us who had made the long voyage home to the U.S.A." In his memoirs, written late in life, he included a moving verse entitled "Ghosts of the Argonne," in which the Fallen (as those who died in World War I were always called) gather at night—to remember:

> Over and over they tell the story
> Of their final charge through the Argonne glade;
> But gathering in by hill and hollow
> With their ghostly tramp on the rain-soaked loam,
> There is one set rule which the clan must follow:
> They never speak of returning home.

Almost all of the verses Rice wrote after he returned home are marked by his wartime experiences. Consider the following lines from "The Final Answer":

> Peace on this war-torn planet? I want it understood
> I like a cheerful neighbor—but give me hardihood.
> Give me the fiber needed to face what lies ahead,
> To make good for the living, to make up for the dead.

"Give me the fiber needed to face what lies ahead" is telling. Rice had come to believe in a Fate similar to that informing the Greek tragedies—and the importance of having the courage to accept it. In "The Winners," he wrote,

> Those only win who reach the gate
> Through surf and storm and bitter gale,
> Through pain and loneliness and hate,
> Through all the sullen thrusts of Fate,
> With battered prow and shattered sail,
> Who look on life and death as one,
> Until the closing race is run.

Rice regarded it as his duty to train a friend "for the ruthless whip of Fate/And build your heart up for the bitter fight." Such training would make it possible to overcome fear, especially the fear of death. In his verses, he returned often to Charon, who in Greek mythology ferries the souls of the dead across the rivers Styx and Acheron, which divide the world of the living from the world of the dead.

> Charon, the day is fading—night is near

Where the last darkness closes out each dream,
And I shall come to meet you without fear
To face the shadows of your silent stream.

He was also fond of quoting these famous lines from Shakespeare's *Julius Caesar*: "Cowards die many times before their deaths;/The valiant never taste of death but once."

Like Rice, the United States to which he returned had been changed by the war. As Frederick Lewis Allen put it in *Only Yesterday*, his classic "informal" history of the postwar decade, "disillusionment . . . was the keynote of the nineteen-twenties." That was particularly true for the intellectuals, especially those who had been at war—members of the Lost Generation—but it affected all Americans. In one of his best chapters, Allen wrote of the revolution in manners and morals, occasioned, in part, by a conviction that life is short and one might as well live it up while one can. Romantic, and responsible, love was therefore out; sex was in. In effect, Allen observed, the liberated woman told postwar man: "You are tired and disillusioned, you do not want the cares of a family or the companionship of mature wisdom, you want exciting play, you want the thrills of sex without their fruition, and I will give them to you." That was all very well, but as Walter Lippmann noted in *A Preface to Morals*, "[I]f you start with the belief that love is the pleasure of a moment, is it really surprising that it yields only a momentary pleasure?"

For Grantland Rice, such a response to postwar disillusion held little or no appeal, but the general cynicism spreading throughout the United States was impossible to ignore. That cynicism increased as a result of the "Black Sox" scandal, in which eight players for the Chicago White Sox conspired to throw the 1919 World Series. For those involved, Rice wasted no sympathy; in his "Sportlight" column of September 30, 1920, he wrote that they were "worse than thieves and burglars. They are the ultimate scum of the universe, and even the spotted civilization of the present time has no place for them outside of a penitentiary." But he viewed the damage that the scandal had done to the world of sport as a whole as yet another instance of tragic Fate.

The 1919 White Sox were the best in the major leagues. The team boasted the game's greatest hitter in "Shoeless" Joe Jackson; an outstanding pitching staff, led by shine-balling Eddie Cicotte; a fine switch-hitting third baseman in Buck Weaver; and future Hall of Famers Ray Schalk (catcher) and Eddie Collins (second baseman). As a result, the Sox were installed as heavy favorites in the upcoming World Series against the National League champion Cincinnati Reds. By the time the Series opened in Cincinnati on October 1, however, eight White Sox players, organized by first baseman Chick Gandil, had agreed to lose in exchange for thousands of dollars from gamblers who would bet on the underdog Reds. The players dealt with a number of unsavory figures, among them Boston gambler Joseph "Sport" Sullivan, former pitcher "Sleepy" Bill Burns, and former boxer Billy Maharg.

More important than those small-timers was Abe Attell, who had once been featherweight champion of the world. Attell was in the entourage of Arnold Rothstein, a wealthy gambler and prominent New York underworld figure. Rothstein later admitted that he knew of the fix and profited from it, but he always denied having put up the money to pay the players off. Nevertheless, belief in his involvement was and is widespread. In *The Great Gatsby*, for example, F. Scott Fitzgerald used Rothstein as the model for Meyer Wolfshiem. Gatsby introduces Wolfshiem to Nick Carraway as a gambler, the "man who fixed the World's Series back in 1919."

Fitzgerald was not alone in his fascination with Rothstein. Rice's colleague and friend, sports writer and short-story author Damon Runyon, knew Rothstein well and liked him—not surprisingly, considering Runyon's sympathy for the gamblers, hustlers, and dispossessed of Broadway; the gambler is a thinly disguised character in a number of Runyon's "guys and dolls" stories. In "A Very Honorable Guy," for example, he is Armand Rosenthal, called "The Brain" (as Rothstein was).

> He is well known to one and all in this town as a very large operator in gambling, and one thing and another, and nobody knows how much dough The Brain has, except that he must have plenty, because no matter how much dough is around, The Brain sooner or later gets hold of all of it.

Whether or not The Brain bankrolled the fix, rumors that the White Sox were going to throw the Series swirled around Cincinnati and Chicago as opening day of the Fall Classic approached. Hugh Fullerton, of Chicago's *Herald and Examiner*, had heard the gossip but did not want to believe it. Still, he and Christy Mathewson, recently returned from the war, decided to keep track of every suspicious play. They did not have long to wait—Eddie Cicotte hit the first batter he faced, a prearranged signal to Rothstein that the fix was on. Cicotte, who went 29–7 during the regular season, had trouble getting anyone out, and the Reds won the opener, 9–1.

In Game Two, the White Sox sent Claude "Lefty" Williams to the mound. For the regular season, Williams went 23–11, with an ERA of 2.64. He pitched well until the fourth inning, when he gave up three runs—the Reds went on to win, 4–2.

Major League Baseball had decided on a best-of-nine format for the World Series, so the Sox were not finished as the teams traveled to Chicago for Game Three. Dickey Kerr, a southpaw who had won 13 and lost seven (with a 2.88 ERA) on the season, took the mound for the White Sox. He was not in on the fix and pitched a fine game, shutting out the Reds, 3–0. The young James T. Farrell, remembered for his *Studs Lonigan* novel trilogy, was an avid Sox fan and attended the game. "No fan around me," he later wrote in his "baseball diary," "gave voice to the suspicion that the two previous games had been thrown."

Cicotte started Game Four, which Farrell also attended, and pitched well through the fourth inning. In the fifth, Cicotte, one of the best fielding pitchers in the majors, picked up a slow roller and threw wildly to first, allowing the Reds' runner to reach second base. The next hitter singled to left, and, according to Farrell, Joe Jackson got off a quick, accurate throw; the runner on second did not try for home, until Cicotte inexplicably cut if off and then juggled it. The Sox went on to lose the game, 2–0, down three games to one.

After Game Five, they were down four games to one; Williams pitched against Reds' hurler Hod Eller, who had won 19 games (including a no-hitter) and lost only nine during the season. He shut the Sox out, while Williams gave up four runs in the sixth; final score, Reds 5, White Sox 0.

The teams returned to Cincinnati for Game Six, and Sox manager Kid Gleason sent Kerr to the mound. The left-hander was not as effective as he had been in Game Three, but he and his teammates were good enough to win the game in the 10th inning, 5–4. With some hesitation, Gleason started Cicotte in Game Seven; no doubt sick at heart, the Sox ace pitched a repentant game, winning, 4–1.

The Series moved back to Chicago, and Gleason gave Williams, who had already lost two games, the nod to try to keep the Sox alive. Farrell was again in attendance and never forgot what he saw:

> In the first inning, Lefty Williams was knocked out of the box, and Cincinnati led, 4 to 0. Jackson failed with men on base in the first inning, but he slammed a home run into the right-field bleachers later in the game. Each time the Sox came to bat, there was hope. But the Reds won, 10 to 5, and the unexpected had happened. The White Sox lost the World Series to a team which seemed to be so inferior to them.

The White Sox were again battling for the pennant in 1920, but rumors of the Series fix continued to fly, and in September a grand jury convened to investigate. All of the suspects, save Chick Gandil who left the team to play semipro ball, had played the season, but all were finally suspended by White Sox owner Charles Comiskey. Under pressure, Joe Jackson confessed to having "helped throw games by muffing hard chances in the outfield or by throwing slowly to the infield." Eddie Cicotte admitted that he "gave Cincinnati batters good balls to hit," adding, "I put them right over the plate." Nevertheless, members of the jury acquitted the players of all charges—for good reason. Judge Hugo M. Friend had instructed them that the law required proof of intent to defraud the public, not merely to throw games. The accused and a great many fans proceeded to celebrate—prematurely, as it turned out.

By August 2, 1921, the day the jury rendered its verdict, the major-league owners had reached an agreement with federal judge Kenesaw Mountain Landis. In an effort to restore public confidence in the game, they appointed the judge the sole commissioner of baseball (replacing a commission composed of the two league presidents and one team owner) and awarded him sweeping powers. Upon learning of the verdict, Landis issued the following statement:

> Regardless of the verdict of juries, no player who throws a ballgame, no player who undertakes or promises to throw a ballgame, no player who sits in a conference with a bunch of crooked players and gamblers where the ways and means of throwing a game are planned and discussed and does not promptly tell his club about it, will ever play professional baseball.

He banned the eight accused players for life.

The banning of two of the players, Joe Jackson and Buck Weaver, has remained controversial. Jackson admitted to taking $5,000 from gamblers but claimed that he never gave less than his all on the field. He hit .375 and played errorless ball in the field, but his average in the five games that the White Sox lost was only .268, and many of his hits came after the game had been decided. Buck Weaver played an outstanding Series, batting .324; he was incapable of playing to lose. But he was present when the fix was being discussed and chose not to report on his teammates. His was the most tragic case.

Despite his considerable knowledge of the world and practiced irreverence, Damon Runyon was stunned by the revelation of a fix. He covered the Series for the *New York American* and had difficulty believing his eyes—but did not seem to suspect the truth. After Game One, he wrote that "Cincinnati's dream came true!" He did say of the Sox, however, "[Y]ou have seen better baseball played in the town lots." After watching Lefty Williams blow Game Two, he could write only that Chicago's number-two hurler "is apt to do better his next time out." Williams didn't, of course, and after the left-hander lost his third game, Runyon wrote in exasperation: "'Couldn't break an egg,' remarked one of the ballplayers, describing the lack of speed behind the ball as delivered by Williams." For Runyon, the game would never be the same.

Nor was it for Ring Lardner, an outstanding sports writer and close friend of Grantland Rice. Lardner wrote for the *Chicago Tribune*, was a White Sox fan, and loved the game—but the Black Sox scandal played to his cynical nature. He had heard the rumors of a fix, and, adopting the semiliterate dialect he perfected in his short stories, he told his readers after the first game of the Series that Chicago's only chance was to "keep the Reds in there hitting till darkness fell and made it an illegal game, but Heinie Groh finely hit a ball that [Oscar 'Happy'] Felsch [who was in on the fix] could not help from catching and gummed up another piece of stratagem."

After the second game of what he referred to as the "present horror," Lardner accompanied the team on the train returning to Chicago for Game Three. After more than a few drinks, he headed for the car in which the players were relaxing with a few hands of poker and burst into song to the tune of "I'm Forever Blowing Bubbles": "I'm forever blowing ballgames,/Pretty ballgames in the air./I come from Chi/I hardly try/Just go to bat and fade and die;/Fortune's coming my way,/That's why I don't care./I'm forever blowing ballgames,/And the gamblers treat us fair."

Eliot Asinof, author of the classic *Eight Men Out: The Black Sox and the 1919 World Series*, sums up Lardner's disillusion in the following way: "His adoration for the White Sox disintegrated; his love for professional baseball began to fade with it. In time he stopped reporting baseball, even stopped going to ballgames." His disillusion was "undoubtedly a contributing element to Lardner's bitter portrayal of sporting figures in his later short stories."

Lardner and Runyon belonged to what in the 1920s came to be called the "Aw Nuts" school of sports writing, one that treated athletes less as heroes than as deeply flawed human beings. Members of the school were as much interested in their subjects' private lives, especially those less exemplary, as they were in their performance on the field of play. Theirs, in short, was the art of debunking, exposing athletes for what, supposedly, they really were. "Not only did Lardner see ballplayers as something less than noble," sports writer Jeff Silverman observes, "he also saw the national pastime as a superb arena to explore and amplify the sour notes of the human symphony."

Members of the Aw Nuts school wrote in reaction to members of the "Gee Whiz" school, whom they regarded as little more than naïve hero-worshipers. As the undisputed leader of the Gee Whiz school, Grantland Rice was often dismissed as a nice man and a good writer who unfortunately belonged to a more innocent era. But this was a serious mistake. Rice was by no means naïve, especially not after having served in the Great War and covered the 1919 World Series. He knew that the great athletes about whom he wrote were imperfect human beings, some very imperfect, but he preferred to uphold their (and by extension our) nobler rather than their baser selves. Or to put it another way: Lardner and Runyon, story-writers both, wrote about the prose of sport; Rice wrote about its poetry.

Granny's writing about Babe Ruth is a perfect example of his resolve to elevate rather than depress the human spirit. He and the Babe were friends for more than 30 years; they played golf together, drank together, and laughed together. In his memoirs, Rice paid tribute to their friendship: "Friendship—pure, warm, unadulterated friendship with no holds barred, ever—is the key to the Babe Ruth I most treasure." He knew, of course, of Ruth's insatiable appetite for food, drink, and women—and so did every other sports writer. W. O. McGeehan, leader of the Aw Nuts school, once referred to Ruth as "our national exaggeration." Perhaps so, but in a "Sportlight" column of March 24, 1948, when Ruth was dying of cancer, Rice balanced the scales:

> The Babe knows the "paths of glory lead but to the grave." He had no worry about a grave. His only thought has been that he will travel the few remaining miles for the betterment of the kids, the cripples, the heart-weary, and the underprivileged, those who might need help and inspiration, as he once needed such help so badly.

Granny wanted his readers to know all this, but even more he wanted them to know that Babe's immortality was due to what he accomplished on the baseball field. "Here, in the way of gold and glory, here in the way of continued thrills, is the greatest man sport has ever known." In the wake of the Black Sox scandal, baseball was near death; almost single-handedly, Ruth brought it back to life with his unparalleled power at the plate. By the time his career ended, he had hit 714 regular-season home runs, an almost unbelievable number.

To be sure, the new "live-ball" era helped make his achievement possible; beginning in 1920, the major leagues no longer used the same ball throughout a game, the spitball was outlawed, and the ball's yarn was more tightly wound. There is no doubt, however, that Ruth was a truly exceptional player and that he, perhaps more than anyone else, made the 1920s the Golden Age of Sport. When he died in August 1948, Rice paid tribute to his friend in verse:

> Game called by darkness—let the curtain fall.
> No more remembered thunder sweeps the field.
> No more the ancient echoes hear the call
> To one who wore so well both sword and shield.
> The Big Guy's left us with the night to face,
> And there is no one who can take his place.

If the Bambino had any rival for preeminence during the 1920s, it was Jack Dempsey, with whom Rice was also—eventually—on friendly terms. In a rare departure from his usual practice of ignoring his heroes' personal flaws, Granny was sharply critical of the great heavyweight champion's failure to serve in World War I. Born William Harrison

Dempsey on June 24, 1895, the future champ left home at the age of 16 and worked as a miner, dishwasher, farmhand, and cowboy while finding his true calling and earning extra money by taking on all comers in barroom fights. Because of his dark hair, he began calling himself "Kid Blackie."

In 1914, Dempsey began to fight professionally, calling himself "Jack" Dempsey, in honor of a former middleweight champion who fought under the name Jack "Nonpareil" Dempsey (although his real name was John Kelly). Wandering from city to city in the West—Dempsey freely admitted to being a hobo—in October 1916, he found himself in Salt Lake City, where he met and married an attractive prostitute by the name of Maxine Cates; the two separated within a year. Nevertheless, when the Selective Service Act—the draft—became law on May 16, 1917, Dempsey applied for an exemption, claiming that his parents, sister, and wife relied on him for support.

At about the same time, Dempsey agreed to take on Jack "Doc" Kearns as his manager; a former boxer and roustabout, Kearns quickly proved that he could arrange fights for his hard-punching protégé. In 1918, Dempsey won 21 of 22 bouts, 11 by first-round knockouts. Kearns judged him ready to challenge heavyweight champion Jess Willard; promoted by the business-savvy George "Tex" Rickard, the match was set for July 4, 1919, in Toledo, Ohio. Thanks to Rickard's skill at hyping an event, public interest in the fight was great. The newspapers sent more than four hundred reporters to Toledo; among them were Runyon, Lardner, McGeehan, and Rice.

Willard had claimed the title by knocking out Jack Johnson, the controversial black champion, in the 26th round of a match held in Havana in 1915. A mountain of a man, he was 6-foot-6 and weighed 245 pounds; Dempsey was 6-foot-1, 187 pounds. Before becoming champion, Willard had killed John "Bull" Young in the ring, but against Dempsey he was fortunate not to have *been* killed. Not able to hear the bell because of the noise from the seats, Willard lumbered to the center of the ring, a straight-up fighter who held his hands low. There he met the bobbing and weaving Dempsey, who launched a devastating assault that left Rice (and everyone else at ringside) in a state of shock. "Never in all the history of the ring," Granny wrote in his report of the fight, "has any champion ever received the murderous punishment which

245-pound Jess Willard soaked up in that first round and the two rounds that followed."

Dempsey put Willard on the floor seven times in the first round. At that time, there was no neutral-corner rule, and the challenger hovered over the stricken giant and did not wait for him to regain his feet before continuing the onslaught. With Willard dazed and unable to rise a seventh time, Dempsey left the ring, believing, along with everyone else, that the fight was over. But officials said the bell had rung before Willard had been counted out. Dempsey was recalled to the ring, and for two more rounds he finished the job of rearranging Willard's face. "If a six-inch shell had exploded against his right jaw," Rice wrote, "it could hardly have changed his features more." The bewildered champion failed to answer the bell for the fourth round.

Granny conceded that the new champion was greater than any of his predecessors—Sullivan, Corbett, Fitzsimmons, Jeffries, Johnson, and Willard—but because of his and others' experiences of war, he could not forgive Dempsey for failing to serve. Yes, he concluded in his column, Dempsey was a champion boxer, but not a champion *fighter*.

> For it would be an insult to every doughboy that took his heavy pack through the mules' train to front-line trenches to go over the top at dawn to refer to Dempsey as a fighting man. If he had been a fighting man he would have been in khaki when at 22 he had no other responsibilities in the world except to protect his own hide.

That is not strictly true; moreover, in 1920, the champion and Kearns were found not guilty of conspiring to evade the draft.

The jury's verdict having (seemingly) exonerated him, Dempsey defended his title twice in 1920, against Billy Miske and Bill Brennan; his first major fight as champion, however, came on July 2, 1921, against French war hero Georges Carpentier (he was awarded the Croix de Guerre and the Médaille Militaire), in Boyle's Thirty Acres, Jersey City, New Jersey. Promoted by Rickard and playwright George Bernard Shaw as the "battle of the century," it produced the first million-dollar gate in boxing history. Rickard, Rice wrote in his memoirs, "cast Dempsey, the scowling, wire-bearded 'draft dodger,' as the villain, with apple-cheeked Carpentier, the amiable, personable soldier boy, as the hero." It was, to put it charitably, a mismatch. Carpentier ran away from Dempsey for three rounds, looking like nothing so much as a scared rabbit. Dempsey put him down in the fourth, and the Frenchman made the mistake of getting back up; down he went again, for the last time.

It comes as no surprise that the cynical Ring Lardner, who covered the fight, judged it to be a sham. In 1921, he published a short story entitled "The Battle of the Century," a thinly disguised account of a fight that was all about hype and money, and little else. Manager "Larry Moon" (Kearns) has a great fighter in "Jim Dugan" (Dempsey), but he can find no opponent credible enough to generate a big payday—until he discovers "Goulet" (Carpentier), a French boxer and war hero. Goulet is quite small and not much of a fighter, but with enough ballyhoo, he is made to appear formidable to a public eager to be taken in. The narrator of the story sums matters up as follows: "The plain facts was this: A good big man was going to fight a little man that nobody knew if he was good or not, and the good big man was bound to win and win easy unless he had a sunstroke. But the little man was a war hero, which the big man certainly wasn't." Lardner did not describe the fictional fight precisely because it was no real contest.

Dempsey did not defend his title again until July 1923, when he won a rather unimpressive 15-round decision over Tommy Gibbons, who, in Rice's charitable words, fought the fight of his life. Two months later, the champ met Luis Ángel Firpo, the "Wild Bull of the Pampas," in the Polo Grounds. In the opening round, Dempsey knocked the Argentine to the canvas seven times with an unrelenting series of fearsome left hooks and right crosses, but Firpo got up each time and even managed to land a right that, with an added shove, sent the champion through the ropes and out of the ring. Whether or not Dempsey was helped back into the ring is still a matter for debate, but Rice, who was at ringside, insisted that reporter Jack Lawrence simply put up his hands to protect himself. "[N]obody, including Lawrence, had to help Dempsey back through those ropes. He was all for helping himself—but fast!"

Early in the second round, Dempsey put Firpo down for the count—and then helped the game challenger to his feet. Rice's lead paragraph summed up the match nicely: "In four minutes of the most sensational fighting ever seen in any ring back through all the ages of the ancient game, Jack Dempsey, the champion, knocked out Luis Ángel Firpo, the challenger, just after the second round got under way last night at the Polo Grounds."

For the next three years, Dempsey stayed away from the professional ring. He settled in Los Angeles, made a series of movies, boxed some exhibitions, married actress Estelle Taylor, and parted ways with Jack Kearns because of a disagreement over money. Only when criticism of his inactivity as champion began to mount did he ask Tex Rickard to arrange a fight for him; the great promoter approached James Joseph "Gene" Tunney, the "Fighting Marine." Although he never saw action, Tunney had enlisted in the U.S. Marine Corps in 1918, and, while in France, won the American Expeditionary Forces light heavyweight championship. After returning to civilian life in 1919, he won a string of bouts by knockout. He fought and defeated Soldier Jones on the undercard of the Dempsey–Carpentier match and told Rice that he wanted Dempsey.

Tunney knew, however, that he had to fight his way into contention if he wanted to meet the heavyweight champion. In January 1922, he beat Battling Levinsky, the light heavyweight champion, and in May, he entered the ring against Harry Greb, a brawler known as the "Human Windmill"; Rice described what followed as "perhaps the bloodiest fight I ever covered." Despite a broken nose and gashes above both eyes, Tunney made it through 15 rounds of a losing effort. He met Greb four more times, winning twice by decision and fighting twice to no decision. In 1924, Tunney fought Carpentier and won when the referee stopped the fight in the 15th round. The following year, he knocked out Tommy Gibbons, never before KO-ed, in 12 rounds. Three more wins and a no decision later, Tunney began training for Dempsey.

Tunney and Dempsey met for the heavyweight championship in Philadelphia on September 23, 1926. A usual, Dempsey was the aggressor, but Tunney was more agile. As the champion lunged forward, the challenger backpedaled while connecting with well-placed punches. When he spied an opportunity, he went on the offensive. "At the end [of the 10 rounds]," Rice remembered, "Dempsey's face was a bloody, horribly beaten mask that Tunney had torn up like a ploughed field." The championship went to Tunney, by decision. When the defeated champion's wife asked him what had happened, he replied with what became one of the most famous lines in sports history: "Honey, I forgot to duck." Years later, President Ronald Reagan spoke the same words to *his* wife after being shot by a would-be assassin.

After his defeat, Dempsey thought of retiring, but Rickard talked him out of it and arranged a match against Jack Sharkey (b. Joseph Paul Zukauskas), the winner to have the right to challenge Tunney. The two Jacks (Sharkey chose the name "Jack" because Dempsey was one of his idols) met in Yankee Stadium on July 21, 1927. The fight was relatively even for six rounds, although Sharkey clearly hurt Dempsey in rounds one and six. In the seventh round, Referee Jack O'Sullivan warned Dempsey about low blows; seconds later, Dempsey hit Sharkey at or below the belt line. Sharkey made the mistake of turning toward the referee to complain—and dropped his guard. Dempsey put him on the mat with a devastating left hook, and the fight was over. "What was I going to do," Dempsey asked unapologetically, "write him a letter?"

Rickard scheduled the Dempsey–Tunney rematch for September 22, 1927, at Chicago's Soldier Field. Before the opening bell, referee Dave Barry reminded both men of the new rule according to which any fighter scoring a knockdown had to move to the farthest neutral corner before the count could begin. In what was largely a repetition of the first match, Tunney was solidly ahead on points through the first six rounds. About a minute into the seventh round Dempsey connected with a left hook to Tunney's jaw and followed it with a flurry of punches that put the champion down for the first time in his professional career. Timekeeper Paul Beeler began the count, but Barry did not because Dempsey had not moved to a neutral corner. By the time Barry led him to the corner, five seconds had passed; Barry then began his count. At nine Tunney got up—he had been down for a count of 14, his head had cleared, and he weathered the round.

In round eight, Tunney knocked Dempsey to his knee and did not move to a neutral corner. Nevertheless, Barry began the count immediately; Dempsey was, however, up at one. At the end of the 10th and final round, Barry and the two judges voted unanimously to award the decision to Tunney. Although he was clearly the better fighter throughout most of the match, he probably would have lost his championship had it not been for the "long count," which has remained an iconic event in boxing—and sports—history.

Grantland Rice knew Dempsey and Tunney well, and admired them both—setting aside the former's draft evasion. But boxing never meant to him what football did. "Boxing," he says in his memoirs, "doesn't deserve to be mentioned with any decent sport. Comparatively speaking, football is in an entirely different setting. It has practically none of the thugs, crooks, cheaters, bums, and chiselers that boxing knows to a large degree." He penned these words near the end of his life, by which time he had become alarmed by the win-at-any-cost approach of many football coaches and players. "A coach that isn't building character should be fired. No matter if he wins every game, he is doing far more harm than good. If football isn't character-building it is no game to be played." It should not, that is, be whether you win or lose, but how you play the game.

That is the way, Rice always insisted, two men high on his list of Golden Age heroes viewed the game of football: Notre Dame coach Knute Rockne and University of Illinois running back Harold "Red" Grange. By the time he died in an airplane crash on March 31, 1931, Rockne and his Notre Dame teams had compiled a remarkable record of 105 wins, 12 losses, and 5 ties; more important, as far as Granny was concerned, the legendary coach had built character in the young men who played for him. Naturally, then, he reveled in the opportunity to cover Notre Dame games—including the famous contest against Army on October 18, 1924.

Notre Dame's backfield that day consisted of quarterback Harry Stuhldreher, halfbacks Don Miller and Jim Crowley, and fullback Elmer Layden; the four young men led their team to a 13–7 victory. In the first paragraph of his column, published the following day, Rice made them immortals.

> Outlined against a blue-gray October sky, the Four Horsemen rode again. In dramatic lore they are known as Famine, Pestilence, Destruction, and Death. These are only aliases. Their real names are Stuhldreher, Miller, Crowley, and Layden. They formed the crest of the South Bend cyclone before which another fighting Army football team was swept over the precipice at the Polo Grounds yesterday afternoon as 55,000 spectators peered down on the bewildering panorama spread on the great plain below.

Badly shaken by the tragic death of a man he admired and was proud to call friend, Granny concluded his "Sportlight" obituary with these sad words: "There are few in this world who can't be replaced. Knute Rockne is one of the few. Here is one wide gap that can't be closed."

What Rockne was to coaching, Red Grange was to gridiron play. Grange grew up in Wheaton, Illinois, 25 miles west of Chicago; as a high-school athlete, he won 16 varsity letters—in football, basketball, baseball, and track and field. For the Wheaton football team, he scored 75 career touchdowns. His family being poor, Grange earned money during the summer by hauling dry ice to homes with iceboxes; when he became famous, he was often called the "Wheaton Iceman." Upon graduation, he enrolled at the University of Illinois, where he played for famed football coach Bob Zuppke.

On October 18, 1924, the day that Grantland Rice was covering the Four Horsemen at the Notre Dame–Army game, Grange gained national prominence in an Illinois–Michigan game. He returned the opening kickoff for a 95-yard touchdown and scored three more touchdowns on runs of 67, 56, and 44 yards—in 12 minutes. Before the game was over, he had scored two more touchdowns, one rushing and one passing; the Illini defeated a powerful Michigan team, 39–14. Chicago sports writer Warren Brown nicknamed Grange the "Galloping Ghost," and the number on his jersey, "77," became famous.

Having missed that unforgettable game, Granny made certain that he covered Grange's last college game, played against Ohio State University on November 21, 1925. The 85,000 fans who attended the game "understood," Rice observed in his column the next day, "that they were looking upon the last amateur run of a backfield star, whose ballyhoo had driven Dempsey and [Helen] Wills from the sporting pages. They were looking upon the final spring of the Galloping Ghost, including all the adjectives you can think of or find in the dictionary."

The fans had indeed watched Grange's "last amateur run," but not his last run; his college career at an end, he quickly signed a contract to play for the professional Chicago Bears, thus providing the pro game with a fresh attraction and new respectability. Failing to get the kind of contract he wanted for the 1926 season, Grange and his agent/partner, C. C. Pyle, took his talents to the new New York Yankees, a team they co-owned. When the Yankees folded in 1929, Grange returned to the Bears, retiring in 1934. Four years later, Arthur Daley of the *New York Times* gave it as his opinion that "professional football, once a shabby outcast among sports, had become a dignified and honored member of the American athletic family."

In a chapter of his memoirs entitled "Football's All-Timers," Rice wrote of the great players who starred in college and with the pros. Three, he thought, stood out from the rest: Grange; gifted Indian Jim Thorpe; and Ukrainian-American Bronko Nagurski, who played for the University of Minnesota and the Chicago Bears. All three played in the one-platoon era—that is, they played on offense *and* defense. The one-platoon system was superior to the now-dominant two (or more)-platoon system. It demanded greater athletic ability and ruled out 300-pound linemen and "special teams," some of which play only on, say, punts or kickoffs. Although Grange was primarily known for his elusive open-field running, "he could also," according to Granny, "block, tackle, and handle passes expertly." He was a complete football player.

After football, Rice's favorite sport was golf, a game he played well and did much to promote—not least as editor of the excellent *American Golfer* magazine. Prior to 1913, golf in the United States was notable primarily for its want of a national hero and absence from the sports pages of newspapers. That began to change, however, when Francis Ouimet, a 20-year-old amateur and former caddy, won the U.S. Open, beating noted British professionals Harry Vardon and Ted Ray in an 18-hole playoff. Ouimet became an overnight hero and went on to a distinguished career, but as Rice put it, his

> dramatic victory over Vardon and Ray in 1913 helped to give golf popular appeal, but it remained for [Walter] Hagen to supply the human interest, to put the throbbing kick into the game. Color, no matter how it's spelled out, means gold for the newspapers. Hagen had more color than a lawn full of peacocks.

Nicknamed "The Haig," Walter Hagen was born December 21, 1892, in Rochester, New York. As a young man, he caddied and worked in the pro shop at the Country Club of Rochester, while learning the game of golf. He turned professional in 1912, and, the following year, finished in a tie for fourth behind Ouimet at the 1913 U.S. Open. In 1914, he won the U.S. Open, the first of his 11 majors. Hagen won the U.S. Open again in 1919; the British Open in 1922, 1924, 1928, and 1929; and the PGA Championship in 1921, 1924, 1925, 1926, and 1927. He earned a great deal of money playing in tournaments throughout the world and exhibition matches with other golfers of note.

Hagen won fame not only because of his skill on the links, but also because, as Rice indicated, his showmanship and flamboyance. A natty dresser who often showed up to play in chauffeur-driven cars, he was unflappable on the course. He once told Rice that he expected to make at least seven mistakes each round, "therefore, when I make a bad shot I don't worry about it. It's just one of the seven." His often-expressed creed was "don't hurry, don't worry, you're only here for a short visit, so be sure to smell the flowers along the way."

In 1926, Hagen, then the PGA champion, challenged Bobby Jones, the brilliant U.S. Amateur champion, to a 72-hole contest, billed as the "Battle of the Century." The first 36 holes were to be played at Whitfield Estates in Florida (where Jones was vice president for sales), and the second in Pasadena, California (where Hagen earned $30,000 a year for "public relations"). Hagen won the match 12 and 11 (12 holes with 11 left to play), earned $7,600, and, in a typical gesture, bought Jones an $800 set of diamond and platinum monogrammed cuff links. Nevertheless, it was Jones who became *the* golfer of the Golden Age, the game's Ruth, Dempsey, or Grange.

Born in Atlanta, Bobby Jones was the son of "Colonel" Robert Purmedus Jones, a prominent attorney. During his years at the *Atlanta Journal* (1902–1906), Rice formed a friendship with the senior Jones and was thus introduced early on to young Bobby. In 1916, as a 14-year-old playing in his first U.S. Amateur Championship at the Merion Cricket Club in suburban Philadelphia, Jones made the quarterfinals—although he displayed an inability to control his temper. Concerned about the boy's indiscipline, Rice nevertheless wrote that, "[A]t his age the game in this country has never developed anyone with such a combination of physical strength, bulldog determination, mechanical skill, and coolness against the test. He is the most remarkable kid prodigy we have ever seen."

During the next seven years, Jones's temperament prevented him from achieving a success commensurate with his talents. "He had conquered golf," Granny wrote in the *Saturday Evening Post* many years later, "but he wasn't able to conquer himself." Eventually he was able to do so, and in 1923, he won his first major championship, the U.S. Open, at the Inwood Country Club in New York. It was, however, a nail-biter. In the final round, Jones shot a poor 76 and ended in a tournament tie with Scottish pro Bobby Cruickshank; the two golfers then met in an

18-hole playoff. They were even as they teed off at the 18th. Cruickshank drove his ball into the rough and chose to lay his second shot up
short of the green. Jones drove his ball onto a patch of dry, hard ground
surrounded by loose dirt; rather than play it safe, he went for the green.
The ball came to rest six feet past the hole; it was, Rice said in the *New
York Tribune*, "one of the boldest and greatest iron shots ever played in
the game that goes back through 500 years of competitive history."
Jones two-putted for a par, while Cruickshank took a double-bogey six.

Jones had only begun. He took the U.S. Amateur title in 1924 and
1925; the U.S. Open and British Open in 1926; the British Open and
the U.S. Amateur in 1927; the U.S. Amateur in 1928; and the U.S.
Open in 1929. He captured nine championships in seven years, but as
his biographer Mark Frost writes, the strain had left him "progressively
more fragile physically and emotionally." In 1930, Jones decided to
attempt a Grand Slam—to win the British Amateur and Open, as well
as the U.S. Amateur and Open. The first stop on the journey was the
British Amateur at St. Andrews in Scotland. After gaining a victory
there, he looked ahead to the British Open, to be played at the Royal
Liverpool Golf Club in Hoylake, England. His victory there was particularly satisfying because he had never before held the title.

Jones was halfway to the Grand Slam. The next challenge was the
U.S. Open at the Interlachen Country Club in Edina, Minnesota. During the second round of the tournament, he hit one of his most famous
shots, the so-called "Lily Pad Shot." At the 485-yard, par five ninth hole,
his drive found the fairway. He pulled out his three wood, but at the top
of his backswing two girls ran in front of him and his shot hit the surface
of the lake in front of the green. Instead of sinking, however, the ball
skipped forward, hit the water again, and ended up on the grass 30
yards from the green. Although eyewitnesses insisted that the ball had
bounced off a lily pad, Jones said it was an event similar to that of a
skipping rock.

Jones went on to capture the tournament and readied himself for the
U.S. Amateur at the Merion Golf Club—the final leg of the Grand
Slam. It being the decade of sports ballyhoo, three radio networks arranged for live hookups and three motion-picture outfits sent crews to
record the event. In the finals of the match play, Jones faced Eugene
Homans, who was not good enough; Bobby played the front nine in
three over par and still was up by three. He was up by seven after the

first 18 holes—and cheered on by eighteen thousand golf fans, including his father, Francis Ouimet, and Grantland Rice. When both golfers parred the 11th hole, Bobby Jones had an eight and seven victory (eight holes ahead and seven to play). He had his Grand Slam.

Knowing that he was not likely to repeat his unprecedented feat and worn thin by the nervous, mental, and physical strain of championship play, Bobby Jones retired from competitive golf; he was 28 years of age. Golf, Rice wrote 10 years later, would never produce another like him. "There is no more chance that golf will give the world another Jones than there is that literature will produce another Shakespeare, sculpture another Phidias, music another Chopin." During those years, Granny's admiration for his friend had grown, and not only because of Jones's greatness on the golf course. There was also the matter of character, demonstrated by his having learned to control his temper and by his sportsmanship on the course.

The latter quality was famously on display at the 1925 U.S. Open, held at the Worcester Country Club, near Boston. Not playing well, Jones came to the 11th hole; his approach to the elevated green fell short and settled in deep grass. As he took his stance, his club head grazed the grass and, in his judgment, caused the ball to move a fraction of an inch. No one saw it happen, but after playing his shot Jones informed Walter Hagen, with whom he was paired, and a tournament official that he was calling a penalty stroke on himself; neither Hagen nor the official could talk him out of it. Although it cost him the tournament, Jones took offense when others praised him for his honesty. As he reportedly put it to a friend, "You'd as well praise me for not breaking into banks."

For Jones, it *was* how you play the game, but that was not all Rice admired in him. Jones was well educated, having earned degrees from Georgia Tech (mechanical engineering), Harvard (English literature), and Emory (law). He was a family man—married and the father of three children. Even more important, perhaps, he remained an amateur when he could have made a great deal of money as a professional. As Mark Frost has rightly observed, amateurism was essential to Jones's self-definition—he practiced law and was a gentleman athlete. Jones was an amateur not in the sense of one who lacks professional skills, but one who plays for sheer love of the game.

After his retirement, Bob (as he preferred to be called) and Granny often traveled together—to golf tournaments, prizefights, and World Series games. "During the early and mid-1930s," Rice wrote in his memoirs, "we made more calls than two sailors," sometimes in the company of their wives, Mary (Jones) and Kit (Rice). In 1936, the two couples sailed to Europe, where Rice was sent by the *Herald-Tribune* to cover the Berlin Olympic Games.

It was not Granny's first Olympic assignment. In 1924, he returned to France to cover the Games of the VIII Olympiad, held in Paris. Like most of his countrymen, he rooted for the U.S. Olympians, many of whom achieved success; they won 99 medals (45 gold, 27 silver, 27 bronze), more than competitors from any other country. Granny derived particular pleasure from the swimming victories of Johnny Weissmuller, an ethnic German born in 1904, in a small town near Temesvár, Hungary (now Timişoara, Romania); he probably did not know that Weissmuller used his brother John's name to compete for the United States. Unlike Weissmuller himself, John was an American citizen. Be that as it may, Weissmuller, who later played Tarzan in the movies, won gold medals in the 100m freestyle, the 400m freestyle, and the 4x200m freestyle relay.

Granny was confident that an American—Jackson Scholz, Charles Paddock, Chester Bowman, or Loren Murchison—would win the important 100m sprint, "[T]he nation that can present a sprinter capable of outracing them to the wire will deserve more than the usual applause." As it turned out, unusual applause was due Great Britain's Harold Abrahams, who beat Scholz by two feet. Coached by Sam Mussabini, Abrahams, who was Jewish, had studied at Cambridge; his victory (and that of devout Scottish Christian Eric Liddell in the 400m) is the subject of *Chariots of Fire*, a film that won the Oscar for Best Picture in 1981. Rice was generous in his praise of both men. Of Abrahams, he wrote, "His sensational performance [was] one of the greatest track achievements ever known." Of Liddell, "One of the greatest runners any nation ever sent to glory."

As a penalty for having caused—or rather having lost—World War I, Germany was banned from the 1920 and 1924 Olympic Games. But, in 1931, while still the Weimar Republic, it won the bid to host the 1936 Games—winter in Garmisch-Partenkirchen, summer in Berlin. By then, however, President Paul von Hindenburg had appointed Adolf

Hitler chancellor, and as Germany's führer the failed artist was determined to exploit the occasion to celebrate the Nazi regime. According to American novelist Thomas Wolfe, "[I]t was as if the games had been chosen as a symbol of the new collective might, a means of showing to the world in concrete terms what this new power had come to be."

Wolfe was in Berlin as an observer, but for those who could not attend, Hitler and Reich minister of propaganda Josef Goebbels arranged to have beautiful dancer/actress/director Leni Riefenstahl film the Games, as she had the 1934 Nazi Party Congress in Nuremberg (*Triumph of the Will*). The imaginative director dug pits, erected towers, and constructed rails for camera dollies, and immersed cameras in waterproof housings in swimming pools. One of her most important assignments was to film *Der Führer* from the most flattering angles. That, to be sure, was primarily for foreign consumption because the Germans required no propaganda shots in the arm. As Wolfe wrote, "[F]rom noon till night [the German people] waited for just two brief and golden moments of the day: the moment when the Leader went out to the stadium, and the moment when he returned."

Wolfe, a Germanophile, was himself overwhelmed by what he described as the "sheer pageantry of the occasion," even though German friends secretly informed him that he was not experiencing the *real* Germany. Of his slightly fictionalized self in *You Can't Go Home Again*, he wrote that "[H]e did not see any of the ugly things they whispered about. He did not see anyone beaten. He did not see anyone imprisoned, or put to death. He did not see any men in concentration camps. He did not see openly anywhere the physical manifestations of a brutal and compulsive force." Neither did Granny, who, however, could not help but notice

> storm troopers, in their severely cut black uniforms . . . looking every inch the super race. You would see them in the streets, out at the jam-packed Reichssportsfeld, at the Hofbraus. They didn't stroll; they marched . . . and gutturalized with the quiet, confident bearing that betokened their Cheshire cat scorn of "less-endowed" mortals.

The Nazi regime put on an impressive show—and so did the German Olympians. They won 89 medals (33 gold, 26 silver, 30 bronze), more than any other country. With 56 medals (24 gold, 20 silver, 12 bronze), the United States finished second in the country standings.

More important, in Jesse Owens the United States could boast of the Games' greatest athlete. Owens won four Gold medals, in the 100m, 200m, broad (long) jump, and 4x100m relay. That was bad enough as far as the Nazi regime was concerned; what made it worse was that Owens was black.

Not every German athlete shared Hitler's obsession with race, however. One of the most moving stories of the Games was that of the friendship that developed between Owens and German broad jumper Luz Long. Having fouled on his first two broad-jump attempts, Owens might not have made it to the finals had Long not suggested to him that he jump from a spot several inches behind the takeoff board. When Owens won the gold, Long, who won the silver, patted him on the back and shook his hand. Owens always regarded Long's act of sportsmanship and friendship as the defining moment of his Olympics, and his life.

In his "Sportlight" column the day after Owens won gold in the broad jump, Rice wrote with some exaggeration that the American practically jumped out of Germany. "It was the day's most spectacular event," an event that Rice would never forget. In his memoirs, he recalls that he had covered track-and-field athletes for more than 50 years, including those who competed in the Olympic Games of 1924, 1932, and 1936. "Of these select world athletes, no one made the impression on me that Jesse Owens did."

Granny was not alone in his appreciation. Everyone who witnessed Owens's feats recognized his greatness. Louis "Louie" Zamperini, the Italian American runner who also competed in Berlin, described his Olympic teammate as "athletic perfection personified." Only 19 years of age when he went to Berlin to run the 5000m race, Zamperini finished eighth, but he ran the final lap in an eye-popping 56 seconds. After the race, he was led to Hitler's box, where an interpreter translated the Nazi leader's words to him: "Ah, you're the boy with the fast finish."

Zamperini's life after Berlin is the subject of Laura Hillenbrand's superb *Unbroken: A World War II Story of Survival, Resilience, and Redemption*. He enlisted in the U.S. Army Air Corps in 1941, and in May 1943, the B-24 on which he served as bombardier crashed into the ocean, killing eight of the 11 men aboard. One of the three survivors died after 33 days adrift, but Zamperini and Russell Allen "Phil" Phillips endured until day 47, when the Japanese Navy captured them. Until the end of the war, the two men, like all Japanese POWs, were treated with the utmost brutality. Zamperini did not recover from his wartime trauma until he embraced Christianity at one of Billy Graham's crusades; he devoted the rest of his life to sharing his faith and inspirational life story with others.

Daniel James Brown points out in *Boys in the Boat: Nine Americans and Their Epic Quest for Gold at the 1936 Berlin Olympics* that, "[I[n the 1930s rowing was the second most popular Olympic event—after track and field." At the Berlin Olympics, held at the regatta course on the Langer See at Grünau, Germany won five of the seven gold medals, but the U.S. crew from the University of Washington took the gold for the men's eights. The victory of the nine young Americans—Joe Rantz, Don Hume, George "Shorty" Hunt, James "Stub" McMillin, John White Jr., Gordon Adam, Chuck Day, Roger Morris, and Bob Moch (coxswain)—has become the stuff of legends.

On the road to the Olympics, coach Al Ulbrickson's boys won the Intercollegiate Rowing Association's National Championship on the Hudson River at Poughkeepsie, New York. In his "Sportlight" column of June 23, 1936, the day following that race, Rice praised the winners for their speed and stamina—the latter, in his opinion, being the most important key to success in sports. Coach Ulbrickson's strategy in Poughkeepsie was the same as it would be in the Olympics—to keep the stroke rate (the number of strokes the crew takes each minute) low, saving crew members' energy for a late sprint to the finish line. The crew, as Rice put it, "had timed its pace perfectly from start to finish—and when the main showdown came, just at the edge of night, Washington had too much left." They finished ahead of mighty California and Navy.

The next stop for Ulbrickson and his Washington crew was Princeton and Lake Carnegie, the site of the Olympic Trials. Six crews were to compete for the right to go to Berlin: Washington, California, Penn, Navy, Princeton, and the New York Athletic Club. On July 4, two preliminary heats reduced the field to four; Washington won its heat easily against the New York Athletic Club and Princeton. The latter crew was eliminated. California won the other heat against Penn and Navy; the latter was eliminated. In the finals, on July 5, the Washington boys again contented themselves with rowing behind the other crews—until it was time to make their move. With 500 meters remaining, Bob Moch told

Don Hume, who set the pace for the other oarsmen, to increase the stroke rate to 40. He did so, and Washington finished a full length ahead of second-place Penn, convincing Ulbrickson that the crew would give a good account of itself in Berlin.

And so it did. With twenty-five thousand fans in the stands, the Washington boys won their preliminary heat on Langer See, although Don Hume, who was crucial to their success, had taken ill. It was not clear that he would be able to compete when the crew raced for the gold against Italy, Germany, Great Britain, Hungary, and Switzerland. In the event, Hume did race, but he was so ill that Moch feared that he might not be able to finish. With Hitler looking on and seventy-five thousand fans roaring, Germany and Italy appeared to establish too great a lead for the Americans to overcome, and when Moch called to Hume to increase the stroke rate he received no response.

Just as Moch was about to tell Joe Rantz to set the stroke rate, Hume recovered enough to perform his duties, and with 350 meters to go, the *Husky Clipper*, as the Washington shell (boat) was called, pulled slightly ahead of the German and Italian shells. In his gripping account of the race, Brown writes that as they neared the finish line, the Washington boys "grasped at shreds of will and strength they did not know they possessed. Their hearts were pumping at nearly two hundred beats per minute now. They were utterly beyond exhaustion, beyond what their bodies should be able to endure." The finish was so close that no one knew at first that the Americans had won, with a time of 6:25.4. Second-place Italy's time was 6:26; third-place Germany's was 6:26.4. One second had separated the three medal winners. Granny thought the race the "high spot" of the Games.

In the spring of 1938, Leni Riefenstahl released *Olympia*, her brilliant documentary film of the 1936 Olympic Games. That the film had a political purpose—casting a favorable light on the Nazi regime—there is no doubt, but Riefenstahl's primary purpose was to create a work of art. In that effort she was highly successful; *Olympia* is always numbered among history's greatest films, its stylistic and technical innovations having had a lasting influence on filmmakers. Aside from recording major events of the Games, Riefenstahl produced a visual celebration of the human body, beginning with gods and goddesses of ancient Greece. Part I of *Olympia*, "Festival of the Nations," takes us from

Greek bodies to contemporary bodies (nude and in artistic motion) to Olympic bodies.

Riefenstahl staged the passing of the Olympic torch from runner to runner, beginning in Greece and ending in Berlin. We see the entrance into Olympic Stadium of several countries, including the United States; Hitler proclaiming the opening of the Games; and the lighting of the Olympic flame. We see German athletes win a number of gold medals, but the "Greek god" of part one is Jesse Owens. We see Owens win the 100m and the 4x100m relay—a study in beauty and grace. With Owens's cooperation, Riefenstahl filmed a re-creation of his winning broad jump. Her depiction of Owens as a god makes it difficult to claim that she embraced Nazi racial notions—in fact, the contrary was true.

Hitler does not appear in part II of *Olympia*, "Festival of Beauty." The festival begins with nude male athletes, all of them well formed, enjoying a sauna. Riefenstahl then shows us gymnasts, fencers, and soccer players. She dwells on the decathlon, won by American Glenn Morris, with whom she conducted a brief affair. Her filming of the University of Washington crew's victory in the men's eights is of particular note; in addition to excellent footage of the actual race, she talked the boys into staging a re-creation of their triumph in order to gain close-ups of Bob Moch (as well as other coxswains) shouting commands into a camera. Her idea yielded spectacular results. The film concludes with diving and swimming events, in which, once again, Riefenstahl emphasized the beauty of the human form.

The same year that Riefenstahl's *Olympia* appeared, 1938, the number-one newsmaker was a small, crooked-legged racehorse named Seabiscuit. Sired by the terrible-tempered Hard Tack, who was himself sired by the great Man o' War, Seabiscuit challenged War Admiral, a son of Man o' War and the 1937 Triple Crown winner, in a November 1, 1938, match race widely regarded as the "race of the century." In *Seabiscuit: An American Legend*, Laura Hillenbrand tells the story of this wonderful horse and his owner Charles Howard, trainer Tom Smith, and jockeys Red Pollard and George Woolf. We learn from her beautifully written account that Seabiscuit's favorite pastime was sleeping and that Smith, having read an article describing the nutritional intake of the University of Washington crew team, saw to it that the horse received feed with a high calcium content.

More important, Hillenbrand tells us that Seabiscuit "seemed to take sadistic pleasure in harassing and humiliating his rivals, slowing down to mock them as he passed, snorting in their faces, and pulling up when in front so other horses could draw alongside, then dashing their hopes with a killing burst of speed." That was exactly what he did to War Admiral in the Pimlico Special match race—jumping to a two-length lead, allowing War Admiral to draw even with him, then breaking away to win by four lengths.

The race commanded the attention of the entire nation, including President Franklin D. Roosevelt. It had dramatic appeal—an underdog and Western upstart (Seabiscuit) trying to defeat an Eastern establishment and heavily favored horse (War Admiral). Sports writers came to Pimlico from throughout the country—Grantland Rice was, of course, one of them. The opening paragraph of his November 3 "Sportlight" column perfectly summarizes the events of race day:

> A little horse with the heart of a lion and the flying feet of a gazelle, today proved his place as the gamest thoroughbred that ever raced over an American track. In one of the greatest match races ever run in the ancient history of the turf at one and three-sixteenths miles, the valiant Seabiscuit not only conquered the great War Admiral, but, beyond this, he ran the beaten son of Man o' War into the dirt and dust of Pimlico.

During the 1930s, Rice, who was then in his 50s, began to experience the loss of friends, to obtain intimations of mortality. Knute Rockne's death in an airplane crash in 1931 had, as we have seen, left him shaken. Then, on September 25, 1933, Ring Lardner, with whom he was close, died at the age of 48. As he often did at such times, Granny sought solace in the writing of verse, in this case an appeal to Charon.

Charon—I speak for a friend—
Wherever the reefs may form,
On to the journey's end,
Keep him away from the storm;
Where the last candle's burned,
Out where the dark is deep—
Give, give him the rest he has earned—
Bring him a dreamless sleep.

Rice suffered another blow when, on May 2, 1939, Lou Gehrig, the great Yankees first baseman, took himself out of the lineup, ending his consecutive-game streak at 2,130, a record that stood until Cal Ripken Jr. broke it in 1995. Doctors at the Mayo Clinic diagnosed the "Iron Horse" with the degenerative disease amyotrophic lateral sclerosis (ALS), now known as Lou Gehrig's disease; he died from it on June 2, 1941. "I have lost countless friends," Rice lamented in his memoirs, "to such diseases as cancer. When the ticket comes up for me or a friend I'd rather it be in the form of an onrushing truck than any form of an incurable, wasting malady. In Gehrig's death, just as with Ruth with cancer seven years later, baseball and Grant Rice lost two irreplaceables."

There was more death to come when the United States entered World War II. Granny championed the American fighting men, especially in his verse. After the victorious battle of Luzon (in the Philippines) in 1945, for example, he "paged" poets of the past, particularly Rudyard Kipling, whom he had discovered in his 20th year. "The meter and jungle drums inherent in Kipling's verse captured my ear and my imagination and never let go," he wrote in his memoirs.

> Kipling, from Valhalla, can't you send me back your pen,
> So I can sing the glory of MacArthur and his men?
> So I can tell the story, where the flames of Luzon burned,
> And send on to eternity the fame that he has earned?

Able to draw upon his own experience in the Great War, however, Rice knew the price of glory, and it was "above the billions."

> We talk about billions we're spending—
> Of billions in gold-minted streams.
> Of billions to bring the war's ending
> And lead us to peace and to dreams.
> But here is the story I'm telling
> Above all the billions that are—
> "We broke through again—but we paid in good men"—
> And that is the price of a war.

The "good men" were almost all young. "All wars are planned by older men," Granny wrote in a poem he entitled "The Two Sides of War."

> But where their sightless eyes stare out
> Beyond life's vanished joys,

> I've noticed nearly all the dead
> Were hardly more than boys.

After the war, Granny's losses continued to mount. On August 16, 1948, Babe Ruth died. That same year, Bobby Jones was diagnosed with syringomyelia, a disease of the spinal cord that causes crippling pain and paralysis. In his memoirs, Rice wrote that Jones was confined to a wheelchair but that "the mental—the really important—side of this great and gracious gentleman shines through with nary a flaw." In that respect, he reminded Rice of Gehrig, "whose dynamic body was short-circuited and snuffed out by another and even more tragic spinal disease."

The loss or the serious illness of friends exacted a toll. Granny continued to write about sports but without the same enthusiasm. "Sport today," he wrote in his memoirs the year before his death, "is much more commercial and much more stereotyped than in my heyday. I doubt if we will ever again have the devil-may-care attitude and spirit of the Golden Twenties, a period of boom, screwballs, and screwball antics. The almighty dollar, or what's left of it, hangs high." He was particularly incensed by what money was doing to his beloved sport of football.

In the May 1951 issue of *Sport* magazine, he published an open letter to college presidents in which he decried the semiprofessionalism of college football and the insistent calls for "victory at all costs" coming from alumni and students. Granny cited the growing size of stadia, the increased cost of tickets, and the ever-larger crowds—all "for an amateur sport supposed to be a minor part of college life!" Naturally enough, the players no longer thought of themselves as amateurs and sought a piece of the action—and many of them got it, one way or another. They were, in fact, semipros, not scholar athletes. If college football programs did not return to a "saner path," they should not, Granny concluded, be allowed to survive. His heart would have been broken had he lived to see the multimillion-dollar spectacle that the contemporary game has become—with an accompanying decline of sportsmanship.

Not surprisingly, Rice devoted many of his columns to the old days. He did not, for example, think that the modern game of baseball could boast of many hitters like Ted Williams and Joe DiMaggio. Old-time pitchers had to face an almost countless number of great hitters: Ty

Cobb, Shoeless Joe Jackson, Tris Speaker, Honus Wagner, Rogers Hornsby, Bill Terry, Napoléon Lajoie, Babe Ruth, Lou Gehrig, and others. In his memoirs he reminisced about "writers and pals"; it is a melancholy chapter. "I believe," he began, "that I came along in gayer, happier times for both newspaper readers and writers." In earlier days columnists had often turned to verse. Rice mentioned in that regard Frank L. Stanton, the popular lyricist who wrote for the *Atlanta Constitution*, and Frank Adams, who wrote for several Chicago newspapers. It was the latter who, according to Granny, wrote one of baseball's few immortal lyrics:

> These are the saddest of possible words—
> Tinker and Evers and Chance.
> Pricking forever our gonfalon bubble,
> Causing a Giant to hit into a double,
> Words that are heavy with nothing but trouble,
> Tinker to Evers to Chance.

Latter day newspapermen—Rice mentioned Westbrook Pegler, Heywood Broun, Walter Winchell, and Ed Sullivan—switched from verse to prose. Obviously, Rice was unhappy about that switch because, "[W]hile sport has been a big part of my life, I must admit that verse has meant even more." And so had friendship; he treasured his memory of the writers with whom he spent long, companionable hours on the road—Ring Lardner, Damon Runyon, Westbrook Pegler, W. O. McGeehan, Jimmy Cannon, Red Smith, and many others. When a friend died, he often expressed his sense of loss in verse—for Lardner, of course, but also for Chicago columnist and humorist George Ade, writer and columnist Irvin Cobb, and novelist Rex Beach. In a long verse entitled "Via Charon, the Ancient Boatman," he remembered a number of the "old guard who recently have beaten us to the border."

Charon came for Granny on July 13, 1954, but not before he wrote his own epitaph—in verse, of course: "'He played the game'—/What finer epitaph can stand?/Or who can earn a fairer fame/When Time at last has called his hand?"

2

THE WORDSMITH

Red Smith

Every newspaperman who worked the sports beat revered Grantland Rice as a man and a writer. "Grantland Rice," Red Smith wrote of him, "was the greatest man I have known, the greatest talent, the greatest gentleman. The most treasured privilege I have had in this world was knowing him and going about with him as his friend. I shall be grateful all my life." In another place, he observed that "Granny wrote of men he loved and deeds he admired and never knew how much bigger he was than his finest hero." These were the considered words of a man widely regarded as the most distinguished sports reporter-columnist in the history of American journalism.

Born in Green Bay, Wisconsin, on September 25, 1905, Walter Wellesley "Red" Smith fell in love with the English language early in life. When, as a student at Green Bay East High School, he recognized that he lacked knowledge of the rules of grammar, he taught himself by diagramming sentences, a discipline that helped make him the out-standing writer he became. After graduating from high school in 1922, he took a year off from school to earn money, but the following year he entered the University of Notre Dame, where he studied journalism and, according to a classmate, "read Shakespeare all the time."

Notre Dame required every student to engage in some form of athletic activity, so Smith joined the freshman track team, coached by Knute Rockne. "He was a great man," the young man from Green Bay recalled years later, "who happened to choose football as a career. It is likely that he would have had exceptional success in almost any other field, for he had exceptional qualities." Not even Rockne, however, could make an athlete of Smith, whose track career ended almost before it began. With the exception of fly-fishing, which became a lifelong passion, his relation to sports would be that of a spectator. It is unlikely that he was at the Polo Grounds for the October 18, 1924, Notre Dame–Army football game that inspired Rice's famous "Four Horsemen" piece, but he did know one of the Horseman, halfback Jim Crowley, who had been one year ahead of him at Green Bay East. Years later he insisted that, at the time, Crowley "was beyond dispute the finest high school player in Wisconsin."

"When I was a boy," Smith wrote in the October 1975 issue of *Esquire*, "it never crossed my mind that I might someday cover sports for a living, but I revered good writers." Admiring Ring Lardner and H. L. Mencken, he began to search for a newspaper job upon graduation from Notre Dame on June 5, 1927. Offered a position as a general assignment reporter at the *Milwaukee Sentinel*, he accepted without hesitation. Although he did not cover sports, he became a faithful reader of Damon Runyon's syndicated columns, which ran in the *Sentinel*. "[H]e was one of the few men of our time," Smith later recalled, "with genuinely original ideas about what words were for."

Always determined to get ahead, Smith contacted the *St. Louis Star* in 1928, and received an offer to work as a copyreader; he accepted immediately and headed for St. Louis. Working at the copy desk was not his idea of a good time, and he was delighted when asked to move to sports. Quickly impressing his superiors, he was assigned to cover the American League St. Louis Browns in 1929. More a punch line than a baseball team, the Browns nevertheless managed a record of 79–73, good enough for a fourth-place finish. For good behavior, his editors assigned Smith to the far better and far more popular St. Louis Cardinals in 1930, and he quickly became a devoted fan.

While still working to develop a style of his own, Smith, like all good writers, borrowed from those he admired—especially Runyon and Lardner. He continued to impress his superiors, who sent him to cover the Cubs–Yankees World Series in 1932; he was in the Wrigley Field press box the day Babe Ruth supposedly called his shot. In the fifth inning of Game Three, the Babe stepped into the box against Cubs pitcher Charlie Root. After the count reached 2–2, he pointed to something: The center-field bleachers? Root? The Cubs bench? No one knew for certain. What was certain was that he blasted the next pitch some 440 feet into the bleachers in right-center, and reporter Joe Williams claimed that the Bambino had called his shot. Smith later said that Ruth "did make a deliberate set of gestures—not a quick, convulsive one—but it did not occur to me that he was calling his shot."

In 1934, Smith had the pleasure of following the Cardinals as they won the National League pennant and the World Series. Styled the "Gashouse Gang" because of their disheveled appearance and rough play, the Cardinals could boast of playing manager Frankie Frisch, shortstop Leo Durocher, outfielder Joe "Ducky" Medwick, outfielder/third baseman Pepper Martin (Red's favorite), and pitcher Dizzy Dean. The pennant race came down to the final day of the season, when the Cardinals faced the Cincinnati Reds; Frisch sent Dean, 29–7, to the mound. Trailing 9–0 as they went into the ninth inning, the Reds loaded the bases on Dizzy, who proceeded to strike out two men and force the third to hit a weak foul fly. Smith concluded his account of the game with this fine paragraph: "Dean didn't laugh. He didn't shout or caper. The man who has been at times a gross clown was in this greatest moment a figure of quiet dignity. Surrounded by his players he walked slowly to the dugout, a mad, exultant thunder drumming in his ears."

Two years later, Smith received a job offer from Stanley Cryor, a former *Star* editor who was news editor of the *Philadelphia Record*; he accepted it because it meant that he would be closer to New York. Soon after arriving in the City of Brotherly Love—and expressing his dislike of his given names—the *Record*'s new man became "Red Smith." A memorable experience came Red's way in early 1937. The *Record* assigned him to the Philadelphia A's spring training camp, which, for that year only, was held in Mexico City. In a suburb of the city lived exiled Russian revolutionary Leon Trotsky, who agreed to sit for an interview.

Smith entitled his interview "Red Trotsky Talks to Red Smith." His sense of humor was further on display in the report itself,

> Fumbling with the writing by which he earns a living, [Trotsky] exhibits all the wild-eyed revolutionary fervor, all the sinister aspect, all the mastery of men, all the compelling powers of oratory, all the irresistible ardor and magnetism of an elderly and not very successful

delicatessen keeper in the Bronx, inking his fingertips over the
month-end statements.

Smith added that he seemed older than his 57 years, "possibly because,
like the very young and the very old, he talks only of himself."

In September 1939, the *Record* rewarded Red for his sports reporting by giving him a full-time column. On the first day of that month,
Hitler sent his armies into Poland, and World War II began in Europe.
Smith knew that more momentous events were occurring on the Old
Continent than on American sports fields, but he thought it no small
thing to remind his readers that there existed a world of bats and gloves,
as well as of bayonets and guns.

It was easier to do that before the United States entered the war in
December 1941. In October of that year, the Dodgers and Yankees met
in the World Series. With the Yankees leading the Series two games to
one, the Dodgers needed a win in Game Four, played at Brooklyn's
Ebbets Field. Leading 4–3 going into the ninth inning, Dodgers hurler
Hugh Casey retired the first two men to face him. Only Tommy Henrich stood in the way of a Dodger victory. With the count 3–2, Dodgers
catcher Mickey Owen called for a curveball; "I tried to hold up," Henrich said, "but I wasn't able to." Larry Goetz, umpiring behind home
plate, signaled strike three, but the ball glanced off the heel of Owen's
glove and Henrich reached first base safely. It went into the record
book as a passed ball. Before Casey could get a fourth out, four Yankee
runners had crossed the plate.

Only in Brooklyn, Smith wrote, "could a man win a World Series
game by striking out." He sympathized with the hard-drinking Casey,
who had entered the game in the fifth inning with the Yankees leading,
3–2, and the bases loaded. He induced the hitting star of the Series, Joe
Gordon, to fly out, "and from there on he fought down the Yankees at
every turn"—only to have "The Thing" happen. The Thing cost the
Dodgers the game and, when they dropped Game Five, the Series.
Thus, poor Owen, who had handled 476 consecutive chances without
an error during the regular season, added his name to the list of baseball's goats.

During the war, Red increased his income by writing for magazines;
in 1944, he sold his first piece to the *Saturday Evening Post*. With a
wife and two children to feed, however, he still found it difficult to

make ends meet. Fortunately, he had a professional admirer in Al La-ney, a sports columnist for the *New York Herald Tribune*, noted for the excellence of its writers. Laney recommended Smith to *Tribune* sports editor Stanley Woodward, who eventually offered him a job as a general sports reporter, although not as a columnist. Still, it was New York, and Red accepted with alacrity; he wrote his first piece for the *Tribune* on September 24, 1945. He impressed the sports staff immediately, and before long, Laney, who disliked the pressure of turning out a regular column, asked that Smith replace him. Red's first column appeared on December 5, 1945, and he continued to write for the *Tribune* until it ceased publication in April 1966.

Smith covered many sports, although he detested basketball and found little to recommend in hockey. Boxing was a particular favorite. "To me," he once wrote, "boxing is a rough, dangerous, and thrilling sport, the most basic and natural and uncomplicated of athletic competitions, and—at its best—one of the purest of art forms." Although perhaps not art forms, the three "wars" between Tony Zale (b. Antoni Zaleski) and Rocky Graziano (b. Thomas Rocco Barbella) were rough, dangerous, and thrilling enough for anyone's taste. In their first match, held at Yankee Stadium on September 27, 1946, Graziano gave Zale what Smith described as a "frightful beating"—until, in the sixth round, he received a blow to the solar plexus that put him down for the count.

In the return match, held in the Chicago Stadium on July 16, 1947, Zale gave Graziano a "merciless beating"—until, drained by the heat, he lost the fight by TKO in the sixth round. The third and final match between the two warriors was held at Ruppert Stadium in Newark, New Jersey, on June 10, 1948. In round one, Tony knocked Rocky down, but he was back up immediately. Rocky had the best of it in round two, but in round three Zale hit him with four stunning lefts, and he had difficulty getting up at the count of eight; Zale then delivered a tremendous left that stretched Rocky out on the canvas, unconscious.

As brutal as the Zale–Graziano fights were, both men survived them. This was not the case for Cuban welterweight Benny "Kid" Paret, who died of injuries sustained in a March 24, 1962, fight with Emile Griffith. It was the third meeting of the two men, Griffith having won the first by a KO and Paret the second by a split decision. In round 12, Griffith unleashed a savage attack on Paret, who slumped helplessly against the ropes. He died 10 days later of massive brain hemorrhaging.

Smith conceded that those who called for the abolition of boxing had every right to cite the Paret case, but he argued that there would always be men ready to fight for prizes and that it was difficult to believe that a "nation bereft of such men would be the stronger or better for it." He also insisted that the abolitionists were less interested in preventing serious injuries than in parading their own nobility. "Some of the fakers now sobbing publicly over Paret have waxed ecstatic over a Ray Robinson or Joe Louis. It must be comforting to have it both ways."

Red counted himself fortunate to have covered some of Sugar Ray Robinson's fights. Born Walker Smith Jr. in 1921, Robinson, who won championships in the welterweight and middleweight divisions, was considered by many boxing aficionados to be "pound for pound" the greatest fighter of all time. He was quick on his feet, had a devastating knockout punch, and could take a punch—by 1951, he had compiled an amazing record of 128–1–2, with 84 knockouts. Moreover, he took on all comers and fought often—19 times in 1950 alone; he had six fights with Jake LaMotta (the "Raging Bull" of Martin Scorsese's famous film), prevailing in all but one.

After taking the middleweight crown from La Motta in their sixth meeting, Robinson embarked on a European tour, during which he lost his title to Randy Turpin in a London bout of July 10, 1951. When he regained it at the Polo Grounds on September 12, Red, along with Joe DiMaggio, Joe Louis, Gene Tunney, and thousands of others, was ringside. He admired Turpin's strength and ability to absorb punishment, and thought the champion had won the eighth and ninth rounds, but when Turpin opened a gash over Robinson's eye early in round 10, the great fighter "opened the throttle all the way." Robinson put Turpin down, but the game champion got back on his feet.

Robinson then began a brutal assault, but Turpin refused to go down again; he was, Red reported, "defenseless, but neither senseless nor altogether helpless." Referee Ruby Goldstein, who had failed to stop the Paret–Griffith bout in time, finally halted the fight. "There haven't been many better fighters than Turpin seen around here in a long time," Smith concluded. "There never has been a pluckier loser."

In June 1952, Sugar Ray challenged light heavyweight champion Joey Maxim in Yankee Stadium's 103-degree heat. Ahead on points, he wilted in the heat and failed to answer the bell for round 14. Knowing that age and a great many fights had taken a toll, Robinson retired and began a career as a song and dance man, but, needing money, he returned to the ring in 1955. After several warm-up fights, he won the middleweight championship (for the third time) by knocking out Carl "Bobo" Olson. In 1957, he lost the title to Gene Fullmer and then regained it (for the fourth time). Continuing to fight often, he met and lost his title (by split decision) to a tough and aggressive Carman Basilio on September 23 of the same year.

The two men met again on March 25, 1958, and this time Robinson gained the split decision—the record fifth time he had won the middleweight championship. The tough Italian was again the aggressor, and Red maintained that he had "won everything but the fight." Sugar Ray, he wrote, "could not have won without the little bit of luck that closed Basilio's left eye like a purple clam." He admitted, however, that it was Robinson who had closed the eye; moreover, the great champion had Basilio in serious trouble in the final round. There had not been another like him in his time, Smith concluded, but "his time is running out, as it must for the greatest and the least of warriors."

Time was certainly running out for Sugar Ray's close friend Joe Louis. Born Joseph Louis Barrow in rural Alabama on May 13, 1914, Louis came of age in Detroit, where he began his boxing career. By mid-1934, he had won 50 of 54 amateur bouts, 43 of them by knockout. He turned pro in July of that year and, as a result of his amateur record, attracted the attention of the men who formed his management team: John Roxborough, Julian Black, and Jack "Chappy" Blackburn (trainer). Louis won his first 22 professional fights, 14 of them by knockout in fewer than three rounds. By March 1935, he ranked among the top five heavyweights.

Despite his meteoric rise to prominence, Louis was unable to find fights that could lead to a championship match. Not only were all three members of his management team black, but memories of former black champion Jack Johnson, notorious for his unconventional behavior and three marriages to white women, constituted a roadblock. As a result, Roxborough signed a contract with Mike Jacobs (who was white) to act as sole promoter of Louis's fights—for 50 percent of his purses.

From among the big-name heavyweights, Jacobs settled on Primo Carnera as the opponent for Louis's first New York match—June 25, 1935, in Yankee Stadium. For one year (June 1933–June 1934), Carnera had reigned as heavyweight champion of the world; he was an imposing

6-foot-6 and weighed in at 265 pounds. The referee stopped the fight in round six, after Louis had knocked the hulking Italian down for the third time. According to the press, Louis was the "Brown Bomber"; more important, most of his countrymen embraced him as an outstanding American fighter, not another Jack Johnson. Upon learning of Louis's death in 1981, Red Smith wrote that from the beginning, Louis possessed a "sense of dignity."

Three months after he dispatched Carnera, Louis returned to Yankee Stadium to meet another former champion, Max Baer. Everyone who was anyone attended the fight—Edward G. Robinson, Cary Grant, George Burns and Gracie Allen, Al Jolson, Jack Johnson, Jack Dempsey, Gene Tunney, Babe Ruth, Ernest Hemingway, and many others. Baer was a dangerous man; two men had succumbed to injuries sustained in bouts with him, and he had floored Carnera 12 times in 11 rounds. He was, however, no match for Louis, who knocked him down twice in the third round; saved by the bell, he could not survive round four. Thanks to Louis's prowess in the ring, his quiet and decent behavior outside of it (he was a womanizer but did not flout it in the Jack Johnson manner), and the growing importance to boxing of national radio, he had become, in the words of his biographer, Randy Roberts, the "most famous black man in the United States, perhaps even the world."

Louis had become the number-one contender for the heavyweight crown, but Jacobs scheduled a final tune-up match with Max Schmeling, a German who had held the title from 1930 to 1932, but had been beaten by Baer in 1933. Few gave him a chance against Joe, who did not seem to take his upcoming opponent very seriously; as it turned out, that was a mistake. A scheduled 15-rounder, the match was held in Yankee Stadium on June 19, 1936. That was two months before the Berlin Olympics, and the same racial drama formed the background—a black man against a member of the superior race. On that night, the German *was* superior. He pounded Louis repeatedly with right hands over the top, before scoring a knockout in round 12; it was Joe's first professional loss.

Embarrassed by the beating he took, Louis quickly won several bouts in a row in preparation for the title bout that Jacobs had managed to schedule (at considerable cost), despite the fact that Schmeling had earned the shot. The champion, James J. Braddock, had not fought since winning the title in an upset victory over Max Baer. Because his career seemed to have ended, forcing him to work on the docks and go on the dole, the boxing world was stunned when Braddock returned to the ring and won a series of three matches against major opponents before outpointing Baer. Because of his remarkable comeback, Damon Runyon dubbed him the "Cinderella Man," the title of a fine film starring Russell Crowe.

Louis challenged Braddock for the title in Chicago's Comiskey Park on June 22, 1937. It was he who drew the famous to the match; among them were Clark Gable, Kenesaw Mountain Landis, and J. Edgar Hoover. The champion was a game fighter, but he was simply not in Louis's league. He caught the better man off balance in the first and put him down—for a count of one. After that it was all Louis. Somehow Braddock survived the seventh round, during which he absorbed a beating, but Louis put him away with a hard right in the eighth, claiming the championship.

But there was still Schmeling. In preparation for a hoped-for return match, Louis fought three men, one of whom, Tommy Farr, the British and Empire titleholder, refused to go down, losing a controversial but unanimous decision. The Schmeling rematch finally arranged, the two fighters prepared for a June 22, 1938, meeting in Yankee Stadium. In what can only be described as a savage beating, Louis battered Schmeling from the sounding of the bell in round one and, with a series of lethal right hands, knocked the German down three times; referee Arthur Donovan stopped the fight after two minutes and four seconds. It was and remains one of the most famous fights in boxing history.

Having promised, when he won the title, to be a "fighting champion," Louis defended successfully 13 times between January 1939 and May 1941. Most of his victims were ranked fighters, but because there were so many of them in such a short space of time, they came to be known collectively as members of the "Bum of the Month Club." They were followed by another of the champion's most famous challengers, the popular and good-looking Irish American Billy Conn. Hoping for the fame and money that the heavyweight championship promised, Conn relinquished his light heavyweight championship to fight Louis. He was a decided underdog when the two men met in the Polo Grounds on June 18, 1941.

The fight was a classic. Conn's strategy was to throw a punch or two and then stay away from Louis, which, when the champion first learned of it, prompted his famous line, "He can run, but he can't hide." In the event, however, Conn fought a smart and winning match; through the first 12 rounds, he was clearly ahead on points. After impressive 11th and 12th rounds, however, he grew overconfident, stopped dancing from side to side, and went toe to toe with Louis. "I'm going to knock this son of a bitch out," he told his manager. Pride goeth before the fall; the champion knocked him out in two minutes and 58 seconds of the 13h round. "What's the sense of being Irish if you can't be dumb," Conn said after the match.

Because of the war, in which Louis served with distinction in the U.S. Army's Special Services Division, a Louis–Conn rematch had to wait until June 19, 1946, in Yankee Stadium. Both men suffered from the long (professional) layoff, but Conn suffered the most. He managed to stay out of range until the eighth round, when Louis hit him with a hard right, then another hard right, then a devastating left. He was counted out at two minutes, 19 seconds.

Three months later, September 18, 1946, Louis defended his title against Tami "The Bronx Barkeep" Mauriello. The challenger staggered Louis in round one, but the champion quickly recovered and knocked Mauriello down with a left hook. Louis ended the match with a series of rights and lefts. Mauriello probably would have been quickly forgotten had it not been for his live postfight radio interview, when, in answer to a "what happened" question, he shocked the national audience by replying, "I got too god-damned careless."

Fifteen months later, on December 5, 1947, Louis returned to the ring against Jersey Joe Walcott (b. Arnold Cream)—both men were 33 years of age. For many rounds at Madison Square Garden, the bout was a slugfest, with Louis stalking his prey and Walcott moving, backing away, and then suddenly striking. He knocked the champion down in the first and fourth rounds, and landed many solid lefts and rights. Louis scored some points with hard rights, but he was clearly losing going into the 15th and final round. Walcott, thinking he had won the championship, stayed out of Louis's reach, a tactic that did not please the judges, both of whom awarded the fight to Louis; referee Ruby Goldstein gave it to Walcott, as did many of those who saw the fight. Most, but not all. Red Smith scored the match even going into the final round and was disgusted by Jersey Joe's efforts to escape a last-minute knockout. "Now Walcott was in full flight. . . . He ducked and danced and ran. . . . He clinched and held; he ran again."

Louis knew that he had performed poorly, but several years later he told an interviewer that if a man knocks a champion down, "he's supposed to come after him. If he don't want the championship bad enough to come and get it, he don't want it bad enough to win it." Not wishing to retire on a sour note, Louis gave Walcott a rematch, held in Yankee Stadium on June 25, 1948. Walcott fought the same kind of fight, dodging, faking, backing away, and suddenly lashing out; he knocked Louis down in the third round, but the champion quickly returned to his feet. Louis continued to press the fight, and Walcott fought less and less until the 11th round, when Louis staggered him with a right, followed by a barrage of lefts and deadly rights that sent his opponent to the canvas. Walcott could not beat the count and, in any case, was in no condition to continue. It was Louis's 25th successful defense, 22 of them by knockout.

On March 1, 1949, Joe Louis relinquished his title and announced his retirement from the ring. He should have ridden off into the sunset, but he could not because he owed the IRS $500,000. He therefore agreed to a Yankee Stadium match with Ezzard Charles, who had succeeded to the heavyweight championship by outpointing Walcott on September 27, 1950. Although he gave all that he had, it was clear from the first round that Louis had little to give. Charles won a unanimous decision, and Louis collected $100,458, not nearly enough to pay his astronomical debt. After facing three second-rate fighters in late 1950 and early 1951, Louis accepted an offer (it turned out to be for $94,000) to fight undefeated contender Rocky Marciano (b. Rocco Marchegiano) on October 26, 1951, in the Garden.

Marciano had compiled a 37–0 record, although only two opponents, Roland La Starza and Rex Layne, amounted to much. He was shorter and lighter than Louis but nine years younger. Not pretty to watch, he was aggressive, could take a punch, and had lethal hands. He went after the aging and flat-footed former champion from the earliest rounds. Fighting from a crouch, he worked his way inside and delivered punishing blows. He missed several wild rights, but in the eighth round he sent Louis to the canvas with a left hook; up at the count of eight, Louis tried to survive the round, but Marciano knocked him through the ropes and onto the ring apron with a devastating right hand. It was the end of the fight and Louis's great career.

Red Smith covered the fight and expressed its meaning as well as anyone, "An old man's dream ended. A young man's vision of the future opened wide. Young men have visions, old men have dreams. But the place for old men to dream is beside the fire."

Of Marciano, Red wrote that it was "difficult to see how he can be stopped this side of the heavyweight championship." At Philadelphia's Municipal Stadium on September 23, 1952, Rocky took the title from Jersey Joe Walcott, who had taken it from Charles on July 18, 1951.

> It was a grand fight, possibly the best for the heavyweight champion-ship since Jack Dempsey's famous "long count" match with Gene Tunney a quarter-century ago. It was a wonderful fight in its own right, close and bruising, and bloody and exciting, but especially good because Walcott's performance was so unexpected.

In round one, the champion knocked Rocky to the canvas for a count of five (the first time the challenger had ever been floored).

It looked to many that the fight might soon be over, but, Smith wrote in praise and wonder, "Rocky had what everybody thought he'd had—courage, great recuperative power, and the strength to throw a killing punch after punishment that would have finished most men." Each fighter delivered punishing blows round after round until, in round 11, Walcott almost put Marciano away. But he didn't, and in round 13 Rocky delivered a paralyzing right hand that, as Smith put it, "separated [Walcott] from his intellect and the heavyweight champion-ship of the world." Nevertheless, those present at Municipal Stadium witnessed "one of the most gallant battles any champion ever made in futile defense of his title."

Red did not have similar words of praise for the rematch, held in the Chicago Stadium on May 15, 1953. With less than one minute left in round one, Marciano knocked Walcott off his feet with a right upper-cut. "There," Red wrote, "old Joe sat like a darkly brooding Buddha, thinking slow and beautiful thoughts while 10 seconds drained away and he made no effort whatever to get up." Old Joe did not, in fact, look as if he were unable to get up. Moreover, as Smith pointed out, he "compounded his own disgrace by putting up no part of a fight during the brief seconds preceding his sit-down strike." It was the uninspiring end of Jersey Joe's long ring career.

Marciano defended his title next against Roland La Starza and scored a TKO. He then fought Ezzard Charles twice, winning the first match on points and the second by knockout. Next he knocked out British and European champion Don Cockell and prepared for what proved to be his final match against 38-year-old light heavyweight champion Archie Moore (b. Archibald Wright). The bout was held in Yankee Stadium on September 21, 1955. Moore knocked Marciano down (for the second and last time in his career) for a count of four in round two, but in the sixth Rocky knocked Archie down twice, for counts of four and nine. He scored another knockdown in the eighth, but Moore was saved by the bell. At one minute, 19 seconds of round nine, Marciano put Moore down for the count.

According to Smith, "by plain strength and courage and resolution, [Rocky] battered down an uncommonly skillful defense, smashed Moore to the floor four times, and scored the 43rd knockout of a career that has never included defeat." Red was particularly impressed by Moore "when he seemed helpless against the ropes, a rolling, weaving turtle with his head retracted under a blizzard of blows." Time after time, the challenger recuperated, but in the end he fell to one of the greatest of heavyweight champions.

On April 27, 1956, Marciano relinquished his title and retired from the ring undefeated; he had compiled a career record of 49–0 (43 of those wins came by way of a knockout). On August 31, 1969, the great champion died in the crash of a private plane. A year later, in a memorial piece for *Women's Wear Daily*, Smith wrote, "[I]t is still hard to believe that he didn't get up." He couldn't, Red said, "box like Tunney and probably couldn't hit like Louis, but in one respect he had no challenger. He was the toughest, strongest, most completely dedicated fighter who ever wore gloves."

In an elimination tournament to find Rocky's successor, young Floyd Patterson emerged the winner, defeating Archie Moore on November 30, 1956. After defending his title against four minor contenders, Patterson faced European heavyweight champion Ingemar Johansson in Yankee Stadium on June 26, 1959. Possessed of a powerful right hand, the challenger knocked the champion down seven times before referee Ruby Goldstein stopped the fight at two minutes, three seconds of the third round. Patterson was not only defeated, but psychologically wounded; as he prepared for a rematch, he was, according to Red Smith, a "deeply lonely man." With the exception of occasional visits, he cut himself off from his family for months, determined to regain his title and self-respect.

Promotion of the return match, Smith wrote wryly on May 16, 1960, "was launched today on a flood tide of oratory, with the announcement that Joe Louis would endeavor to teach Floyd to do unto Ingemar as Joe did unto Max Schmeling after the German had knocked him out." The bout was held in the Polo Grounds on June 20. From the opening bell, Patterson was the aggressor, a man possessed. Johansson landed a solid right in round two, but otherwise it was all Patterson. In round five he knocked the champion down with a left hook; he struggled to his feet at the count of nine, but at one minute, 51 seconds Patterson delivered a swinging left that knocked Johansson out cold. It was five minutes before anyone could revive him. Smith described what he had witnessed as follows: "Ten minutes after the fight they scraped Ingemar Johansson off the floor, propped him on a stool, bundled him in white like a sore thumb, and nudged him gingerly into his first step on the long road back to Göteborg."

In his last column, dated January 11, 1982, Smith reported that one of the questions he was asked repeatedly was, "Of all those you have met, who was the best athlete?" He thought the question unanswerable, but jockey Bill Shoemaker always came to his mind. "The little guy weighed 96 pounds as an apprentice rider 32 years ago. He still weighs 96 pounds, and he will beat your pants off at golf, tennis, and any other game where you're foolish enough to challenge him." In a piece he wrote in 1970, he was less hesitant: "Pound for pound, [Shoemaker's] got to be the greatest living athlete." In his 40s, "Shoe" was tested at the National Athletic Health Institute; he was found to be in the top 10 percent of mature athletes in power, endurance, and muscle strength. During a long career in his chosen profession, the 4-foot-11 athlete rode 8,833 winners. Smith witnessed his share of them, in part because it was his job, but also because he loved thoroughbred racing.

Among other jockeys Red admired were Eddie Arcaro and George ("Georgie") Woolf, who rode Seabiscuit to victory over War Admiral. It was not only their talent that impressed him, but their courage; he knew the profession those men had chosen was a dangerous one. When

Woolf died after being thrown from his mount (who may or may not have stumbled), Smith reminded his readers, "[E]very time one of these little guys scrambles into the saddle for a race he is literally taking his life in his hands"; he did not exaggerate.

And then, of course, there were the horses themselves. In 1948, the great Citation won the Triple Crown, and Red watched him claim the Kentucky Derby, with Arcaro aboard. There was never any doubt about the outcome of the race, he wrote, but "for those to whom it means something just to see an exceptional horse in a spectacular setting, it was as good as a race could possibly be." Citation "was so very, very good, he ran his race so willingly in such tractable obedience to Eddie Arcaro's guidance, [and] he won with such indisputable ease."

Several years earlier, on March 2, 1940, Red watched as Seabiscuit won the Santa Anita Handicap. Seventy-eight thousand fans from throughout the nation gathered to see the beloved horse race for what proved to be the last time. In the luxury boxes, one could glimpse such celebrities as Clark Gable and Carole Lombard, Jack Benny, Sonja Henie, James Stewart, and Bing Crosby. In the press box with Red were reporters from around the world. Radios in every corner of the globe were tuned to the broadcast of the race.

With Red Pollard in the saddle, Seabiscuit, carrying 130 pounds, powered out of the gate. Whichcee took an early lead, and after the final turn he and Wedding Call formed a wall in Seabiscuit's path, before separating just enough to open a small hole. Seabiscuit surged through it into the lead. Kayak (also from the Charles Howard stable) mounted a final challenge, and Seabiscuit again eased up before breaking free and winning by one-and-a-quarter lengths in record time. Smith confessed to having a soft spot for Seabiscuit after the match with War Admiral (the "best horse race these eyes have seen"), but he was among those who claimed that Kayak could have won the race had Howard wanted it so.

Laura Hillenbrand has refuted the claim persuasively. She quotes George Woolf, who had ridden both horses, who said, "[I]f Kayak had charged at him . . . [Seabiscuit] would have bounded away. . . . That fellow never saw the day when he could take the champ." Even if Buddy Haas, who rode Kayak, had held the horse back (which he denied privately to Charles Howard), it does not follow that Seabiscuit could have been overtaken. "It may have seemed that [Kayak could have won]," Red Pollard said, "but you have to ride Seabiscuit to know him. No horse is ever going to pass him once he gets to the top and the wire is in sight. . . . A horse racing alongside him just makes him run all the harder."

Despite his skepticism, Smith frowned on any thought of a Seabiscuit–Kayak match race, convinced that the "Old Man has earned his pension." After some hesitation, Howard agreed; he retired Seabiscuit. Hillenbrand sums up the famous horse's achievements:

> In six years, Seabiscuit had won 33 races and set 13 track records at eight tracks over six distances. He had smashed a world record in the shortest of sprints, one-half mile, yet had the stamina to run in track record time at one and five-eighths miles. Many of history's greatest horses had faltered under 128 pounds or more; Seabiscuit had set two track records under 133 pounds and four more under 130, while conceding massive amounts of weight to his opponents.

Seabiscuit lived out his life at Ridgewood Ranch near Willits, California; he died on May 17, 1947. "Let's talk about the death of Seabiscuit," Red wrote,

> If someone asked you to list horses that had, apart from speed or endurance, some quality that fired the imagination and captured the regard of more people than ever saw them run, you'd have to mention Man o' War and Equipoise and Exterminator and Whirlaway and Seabiscuit. And the honest son of Hard Tack wouldn't be last.

Horse races and boxing matches are episodic events, but baseball games are played almost daily during the span of a long season. Moreover, baseball in the 1940s and 1950s was still the national pastime. It comes as no surprise, then, that Red Smith wrote a great many pieces about the game. He had little choice. New York, to which he repaired in 1945, was home to three major-league teams—the Yankees, Giants, and Dodgers. They were soon to dominate the game; Roger Kahn entitled one of his books *The Era, 1947–1957: When the Yankees, the Giants, and the Dodgers Ruled the World.*

"The Era" had not quite begun in 1946, the season in which baseball renewed itself (after the years of war) and gave fans a thrilling seven-game World Series between the St. Louis Cardinals and Boston Red Sox. Covering the Series was like Old Home Week for Smith, who, we recall, had covered the Cardinals when he worked at the *St. Louis Star.* Almost as though he knew in advance what was going to happen in Game Seven, he devoted a piece to Cardinals outfielder Enos "Country" Slaughter on the eve of that deciding matchup. "When," he wrote, "you add up the factors that make a ballplayer great, when you consider hitting, fielding, running, throwing, hustle, and the combative spirit that pays off biggest when the pressure is heaviest, Slaughter scores more points than any other" man on either team.

He certainly did in Game Seven. The two teams were knotted at three going into the bottom—the St. Louis—half of the eighth inning. Red Sox right-hander Bob Klinger began by giving up a single to Slaughter, but he managed to retire the next two batters. The count on Harry "The Hat" Walker was 2–1 when the left-handed hitter poked a hit over shortstop Johnny Pesky's head into left-center field. What followed is one of the most discussed moments in World Series history.

Slaughter was off and running with the pitch to Walker and never hesitated as he rounded the bases. Instead of firing the ball home, centerfielder Leon Culberson, in for the injured and more talented Dom DiMaggio, lobbed a relay to Pesky, whose back was to the infield. Because of the roar of the crowd, the shortstop could not hear cries to hurry his throw. He *seemed* to hold the ball for a moment before firing it several feet up the line toward third. Slaughter slid home, unmolested. His "Mad Dash" put the Cardinals ahead to stay, and Pesky, never a shirker, accepted full blame.

Red's sense of humor was on display in his account of Slaughter's heroics.

> Pesky, still out behind second, stood morosely studying [National League president] Ford Frick's signature on the ball. His interest was natural, for the ball he's accustomed to play with is signed by [American League president] Will Harridge. At length he turned dreamily, gave a small start of astonishment when he saw Slaughter halfway home, and threw in sudden panic. The throw was weak. Roy Partee, the catcher, had to take a step or so from the plate, and as he caught the ball Slaughter slid in behind him.

Smith concluded that he had witnessed one of the most exciting World Series games ever played. Some, he said, compared it to the seventh game of the 1926 Series, which Grover Cleveland Alexander saved for the Cardinals by striking out Yankees second baseman Tony Lazzeri with the bases filled. He himself was among the "some," because he had recalled the game only two months earlier in a memorial piece on Lazzeri, who died at the age of 42 from a fall resulting from a heart attack. "It was Lazzeri's misfortune," he wrote then, "that although he was as great a ballplayer as ever lived, the most vivid memory he left in most minds concerned the day he failed." He was unable to resist recounting that someone asked Alexander how he felt when Lazzeri struck out. "How did I feel?" the great alcoholic hurler snorted. "Go ask Lazzeri how he felt."

"The Era" began in 1947, a year in which the Yankees defeated the Dodgers in a seven-game World Series famous for two dramatic moments. In Game Four, played at Ebbets Field, Yankees hurler Bill Bevens (7–13 on the year) walked 10 Dodgers but allowed no hits for eight and two-thirds innings. With his team leading, 2–1, and Dodger pinch-runner Al Gionfriddo on first, Bevens was on the verge of pitching the first no-hitter in World Series history. The gifted but injury-prone Pete Reiser came to the plate to bat for pitcher Hugh Casey. With the count 2–1, Gionfriddo broke for second and slid headfirst under catcher Yogi Berra's throw; the pitch from Bevens had been high, and the count on Reiser stood at 3–1.

Yankees manager Bucky Harris then decided, against the conventional wisdom, to walk Reiser, putting the potential winning run on base. Dodgers manager Burt Shotton called upon Cookie Lavagetto to hit for Eddie Stanky. Lavagetto swung and missed the first offering from Bevens before lining a double to the wall in right-center that drove home two runs and gave the Dodgers a 3–2 victory. "Dodgers," Red wrote, "pummeled Lavagetto. Gionfriddo and [Eddie] Miksis [running for Reiser] pummeled each other. Cops pummeled Lavagetto. Ushers pummeled Lavagetto. Ushers pummeled each other." According to the great Dodgers centerfielder Duke Snider, Red did not much care for the Dodgers.

In an interview that he gave late in life, Red offered a different explanation for his mocking sentences; he said that he always tried to remember "that sports isn't Armageddon. These are just little games that little boys can play, and it really isn't important to the future of civilization whether the Athletics or the Browns win." That is why he almost always found something humorous about baseball games, even those played in the World Series. The piece on the Lavagetto–Bevens game contains one of his most famous lines. In the eighth inning, Dodgers outfielder Gene Hermanski hit a drive to the scoreboard. Yankees outfielder Tommy Henrich leaped for it, "either four or 14 feet into the air. He stayed aloft so long he looked like an empty uniform hanging in its locker. When he came down he had the ball."

The Yankees led the 1947 Series three games to two as Game Six began in Yankee Stadium. The Dodgers scored four times in the top of the sixth and took an 8–5 lead. In the home sixth, with two men on and two outs, Joe DiMaggio came to the plate and belted a long drive that looked to be a three-run homer, until Al Gionfriddo, in for defensive purposes, made a historic catch at the bullpen fence in left. In a rare display of emotion, the "Yankee Clipper" kicked the dirt as he approached second base. Years later, he praised Gionfriddo for making the "greatest catch that anybody ever made in the whole history of baseball." Not so, said Red Smith, who turned the catch into a joke:

> There were 74,065 customers in the yard, including the 65 who had heard Gionfriddo's name before the Series started. Now he has two legs on a pedestal at Cooperstown. Running in frenzied, hopeless pursuit of DiMaggio's drive, Al twisted to look back so often that he got himself wound up like a yo-yo. Somehow, a step or so short of the bullpen gate, he unwound himself and stole three runs from the Yankees.

The Dodgers went on to win the game, 8–6, forcing a Game Seven. Smith noted that the Yankees were favored because they had the pitching—and then pointed out mockingly that they had Bill Bevans ready, a "guy who loses no-hitters." Bevens did pitch in relief and gave up a run, but the Yankees, behind the relief pitching of Joe Page, won the game, and hence the Series, 5–2. None of the men who gained a measure of fame in the Series—Bevens, Lavagetto, and Gionfriddo—ever played in another major-league game.

Baseball and the men who played it were not always sources of humor for Red Smith. He did not joke when he wrote of the courage displayed by Branch Rickey (whom he greatly admired) and Jackie Robinson, who together broke baseball's color line, or when, in August 1948, he penned a moving tribute to Babe Ruth, who had succumbed to cancer. He thought it unfortunate that the Babe would likely be remembered only for his home runs. He was also, Red reminded his readers, "a genuinely great pitcher, a genuinely great outfielder, a genuinely great competitor, a truly great personality." There would never, he concluded, as Granny Rice had, be another like him.

The idea that one should not rate a ballplayer by his separate talents, but by their sum, appears often in Smith's work. It was on that basis, for example, that he wrote in January 1948, that no player of Joe DiMaggio's time could rival him. That opinion was shared by Ernest Hemingway, whom Smith met at Toots Shor's saloon in the late 1940s. "I must be worthy of the great DiMaggio, who does all things perfectly," says the old man in Hemingway's *The Old Man and the Sea*. It is likely, in fact, that the famous author, an old journalist himself, formed his opinion partly as a result of reading Red Smith. He suggests as much in *Across the River and into the Trees*, the novel he published in 1950.

The book concerns Colonel Richard Cantwell, a middle-aged U.S. infantry officer who experienced the horrors of World War II in Europe and suffers from what is certain to be terminal heart disease. In Venice, he finds love with an Italian countess still in her teens, although he knows it cannot last. At one point in the novel, Colonel Cantwell picks up the Paris edition of the *New York Herald Tribune*. "He was reading Red Smith," Hemingway wrote, "and he liked him very much."

Joe DiMaggio retired at the close of the 1951 season. "When baseball is no longer fun," he said, "it is no longer a game. . . . And so, I have played my last game of ball." That, Smith wrote, "is the amateur view. It is the feeling which prevents a great commercial enterprise like baseball from ever becoming a commercial enterprise exclusively." The favorable press that Red gave DiMaggio, whom he knew from convivial meetings at Toots Shor's, earned him a reprimand from Stanley Woodward. He told Smith he was "*not* writing about deities. Stop godding up the athletes." Red never forgot it, and that may account for his often-mocking tone. Late in life, he told Jerome Holtzman in an interview that he "tried not to exaggerate the glory of athletes. . . . But I'm sure I have contributed to false values—as Stanley Woodward said, 'Godding up those ballplayers.'"

As Yankee good fortune would have it, the Yankee Clipper's final season was the first season for his successor in center field, Mickey Mantle. Mantle was then a 19-year-old whom everyone recognized as the "natural" he was. Red quoted former Yankees great Bill Dickey, who said of him, "He's green, but he's got to be great. All that power, a switch-hitter, and he runs like a striped ape. If he drags a bunt past the pitcher, he's on base. I think he's the fastest man I ever saw with the Yankees."

Mantle could, in fact, sprint from home to first in 3.1 seconds when swinging from the left side—despite the fact that he suffered from osteomyelitis, a dangerous bone disease, and sustained a serious knee injury in the 1951 World Series. He had huge forearms and could rifle the ball from anywhere in the outfield. During the course of his career, he hit 536 home runs, some of which were orbital. On April 17, 1953, he unloaded on a pitch from Washington left-hander Chuck Stobbs. The ball clipped a beer sign on its way out of Griffith Stadium and came to rest in a backyard, 565 feet away; it inspired the expression "tape-measure home run." His career batting average was .298.

Perhaps because he was playing in the shadow of the great DiMaggio in 1951, the "Mick's" rookie numbers were relatively modest: 13 home runs, 65 RBIs, and a .267 batting average. He struck out 74 times and had to spend a month with the minor-league Kansas City Blues, with whom, however, he hit .364, with 11 home runs and 50 RBIs in 40 games.

What was worse for the ballclub, DiMaggio's numbers for the season were almost precisely the same as Mantle's: 12 home runs, 71 RBIs, and a .263 batting average (the lowest of his career). No Yankee regular hit .300. No one drove in 100 runs. No one hit 30 home runs. And yet the Yankees won the pennant. The primary reason for their success, as Sol Gittleman points out in his collective biography, was the performance of three pitchers (and close friends): Eddie Lopat (b. Edmund Walter Lopatynski), the "Junkman," who compiled a record of 21–9; Vic Raschi, a fireballer who went 21–10; and Allie Reynolds, another hard thrower who won 17, lost 8, and saved 7.

Reynolds was one-quarter Creek Indian and had been a baseball, track, and football star at Oklahoma A&M. Drafted by the football New York Giants, he chose baseball as a career and signed a contract with the Cleveland Indians. At the time of the Japanese attack on Pearl Harbor, he was married and the father of three children—hence ineligible for enlistment or the draft. Late in the 1942 season, the Indians summoned him from the minor leagues. Although he compiled an 18–12 record in 1945, he slipped to 11–15 in 1946, and the Indians gave up on him; on October 11, 1946, they traded him to the Yankees for second baseman Joe Gordon. They soon had reason to regret it. Reynolds went 19–8 in 1947, his first year as a Yankee, and continued his winning ways in 1948, 1949, and 1950 (although he had bone chips in his elbow in the latter year).

On July 12, 1951, Reynolds, who still had bone chips in his elbow, pitched a no-hitter against the Indians and the great Bob Feller, who had thrown a no-hitter of his own on July 1. Scheduled to play a Yankee Stadium doubleheader against the Red Sox on Friday, September 28 ("American Indian Day"), the Yankees needed a victory to clinch at least a tie for the pennant; manager Casey Stengel sent Reynolds to the mound in the first game. He took an 8–0 lead, and a no-hitter, into the ninth inning. Amused by the fact the "noble redman" was on the verge of making history on American Indian Day, Red Smith described what happened next. A pinch-hitter named Charley Maxwell grounded out. Dom DiMaggio (Joe's brother) walked. Johnny Pesky took a called third strike; there was one out to go, but it was in the person of Ted Williams. Reynolds's first pitch to the "Splendid Splinter" was a called strike. Williams popped up the second pitch behind home plate. According to Smith, a slight wind swept the ball back over Yogi Berra's head; he missed the catch and fell to the ground.

"Yogi didn't want to get up," Red wrote. "He wanted to keep going down, into a hole, out of sight. The game should be over, and now, if Williams should get a hit on this second chance—." Knowing how his catcher felt, Reynolds told him, "Don't worry, Yog. We'll get him again." And so they did. Williams lifted the next pitch foul in front of the Yankees dugout, and Yogi caught it for Reynolds's second no-hitter of the season. No American League pitcher had ever performed the feat before; in the National League, Johnny Vander Meer had thrown two consecutive no-hitters in 1938.

In 1951, National League fans witnessed the most dramatic pennant race in baseball history—between the Dodgers and the Giants. "Everybody conceded the Dodgers' superiority," Smith observed in a column of September 30. They had Gil Hodges at first base, Jackie Robinson at second, Billy Cox at third, Pee Wee Reese at shortstop, Roy Campanella behind the plate, Andy Pafko in left field, Duke Snider in center, and Carl Furillo in right. Don Newcombe, Carl Erskine, and Ralph Branca were the mainstays of the pitching staff. Smith found little to praise in

Leo Durocher's Giants, although that may have been by way of criticizing the Dodgers for having failed to maintain the 13-and-a-half-game lead they held on August 11. They did have rookie sensation Willie Mays in center field and Don Mueller in right; Monte Irvin, like Mays a former Negro Leaguer, patrolled left. At first base was Whitey Lockman, at second the "brat," Eddie Stanky. Alvin Dark, master of the art of hitting behind the runner, was the shortstop. To make room for Mays, Durocher had moved Bobby Thomson to third base. Wes Westrum handled the catching for a pitching staff anchored by Sal "The Barber" Maglie, Larry Jansen, and Jim Hearn.

The Giants may have looked finished on August 11, but then the charge began. In their final 44 games, they notched 37 victories. While they surged, the Dodgers struggled. They won only 24 of their last 44. At the end of the regular season, therefore, each team had a record of 96–58. For only the second time in its history, the National League prepared for a playoff series—best-of-three. "It doesn't matter," Red wrote, "whether you admire Leo Durocher's taste in haberdashery or not; you needn't applaud his diction or concur with his views on world affairs or approve of his social graces. You must accept him as the manager and leader of the team that has brought off this magnificent coup." He could not resist adding the following: "It would be a more agreeable world to live in if the cult of Dodger worshippers were just a mite less vociferous in their protestations of idolatry."

To Smith's evident delight, the Giants captured the first game of the playoffs, played at Ebbets Field, 3–1; the Dodgers took the second, at the Polo Grounds, 10–0. The entire season thus came down to a final game at the Polo Grounds. Dodgers skipper Charlie Dressen sent Newcombe to the mound, while Durocher handed the ball to Maglie. With the score knotted at one, the Dodgers rallied for three in the eighth and led, 4–1, going into the last of the ninth; the "Boys of Summer" (as Dodgers fan Roger Kahn has called them) needed only three more outs. Giants fans began to come alive when Alvin Dark led off the inning with a single off Hodges's glove and advanced to third on Mueller's hard-hit single through the spot where Hodges, who had inexplicably been told by Dressen to hold Dark on, should have been playing. When Monte Irvin fouled out, hope dwindled, but all was not yet lost. Whitey Lockman laced Newcombe's second pitch down the line in left, and by the time Andy Pafko retrieved and fired the ball back to the infield, Dark had scored. Mueller broke his ankle sliding into third; Clint Hartung ran for him, and the tying runs were in scoring position as Bobby Thomson walked to the plate.

Dressen removed Newcombe, who was about to collapse from fatigue. Now he had a crucial decision to make. Should he call on Clem Labine, who had pitched game two, or the more experienced Carl Erskine? In the end, he relied on pitching coach Clyde Sukeforth's judgment and summoned Ralph Branca, who had served a gopher ball to Thomson in game one of the series. Smith told his readers what happened next with one of his finest and most memorable paragraphs: "Now it is done. Now the story ends. And there is no way to tell it. The art of fiction is dead. Reality has strangled invention. Only the utterly impossible, the inexpressibly fantastic, can ever be plausible again."

Branca started Thomson off with a fastball strike on the inside corner. His next pitch was up and in, but Thomson leaned back and connected. Pafko raced to the 17-foot wall in left—and never forgot what he saw. "It was a hard shot, right down the line," he said. "I wasn't aware at first that it was going in for a homer. But when it passed over my head, the whole thing became a terrible blur. I had the best view of it of anyone in the house—and wish I hadn't." The time was 3:58 p.m. on the East Coast. Pandemonium ensued. A Brooklyn man taped Giants broadcaster Russ Hodges as he shouted into the microphone, "The Giants win the pennant, the Giants win the pennant, the Giants win the pennant, the Giants win the pennant. . . . I don't believe it, I don't believe it, I do not believe it." Probably the most famous call in history. Red ended his piece with these words: "Ralph Branca turned and started for the clubhouse. The number on his uniform looked huge. Thirteen."

According to Smith, "magic and sorcery and incantation and spells has taken the Giants to the championship of the National League and put them into the World Series." Could they work another miracle against the Yankees? Behind Dave Koslo, they beat Allie Reynolds and the Yankees, 5–1, in Game One, played in Yankee Stadium. In Game Two, also played in Yankee Stadium, Eddie Lopat and the Yankees beat Larry Jansen, 3–1. The two teams then moved from the Bronx to Manhattan, where the Giants' Jim Hearn beat Vic Raschi, 6–2. Perhaps they still had the magic. Still in the Polo Grounds, the Yankees, behind Reynolds, evened the Series, 6–2; Sal Maglie suffered the loss. In the final game in the Polo Grounds, Yankee hitters made it easy for Lopat, 13–1; Jansen took the loss.

Back in Yankee Stadium for Game Six, Raschi faced Koslo. The teams were tied at one after five, but in the sixth Hank Bauer hit a bases-loaded triple to put the Yankees in the lead, 4–1. Eddie Stanky singled to start the Dodger ninth inning. Dark then bunted safely, and Lockman singled, loading the bases with no outs; right-handed hitter Monte Irvin came to the plate. Stengel then took the ball from right-hander Johnny Sain (in relief of Raschi), which made sense, and gave it to left-hander Bob Kuzava, which didn't. Irvin scored Stanky with a long fly, and Thomson scored Dark with another fly ball. That made the score 4–3, with the tying run in scoring position on second base. Pinch-hitter Sal Yvars hit the first pitch on the line to right; as Red told it amusingly, Bauer's "feet shot from under him as he made the catch. But he held the ball, and as his bottom hit the turf, the bottom dropped out of the Hasheesh market." The Yankees were world champions again. "Well," Smith concluded, "the nonsense had gone far enough."

"Kuzava," Red wrote in October 1952, "is a Polish name that sounds like some kind of melon." Perhaps so, but what is certain is that he reprised his pivotal 1951 role in the 1952 World Series between the Yankees and Dodgers. The Series was tied at three games each when the two teams faced each other in the seventh and deciding match, played in Ebbets Field. The Yankees took a 4–2 lead into the bottom of the seventh. With one out, the Dodgers filled the bases off Vic Raschi (in for Reynolds, who was in for Lopat); Stengel then called upon Kuzava, who induced Duke Snider to pop out. With the count 2–2, Jackie Robinson hit a high popup that should have been an easy out. But neither Kuzava nor first baseman Joe Collins, who lost the ball in the sun, made a move toward the spot between the mound and first base, where the descending sphere was headed.

It was the kind of moment on the field that delighted Red Smith. Collins, he wrote in his report of the game, "stood gazing curiously aloft, wondering about life. Billy Martin, the second baseman, stood gazing curiously at Collins, wondering about him. For what seemed a full week, nobody moved. In fact, Collins still hasn't." As Dodger runners were rounding the bases, Martin raced forward and caught the ball a few inches from the ground. "I had nightmares for two or three months," Collins said later. "I can see that ball dropping and losing the

World Series." With the scare behind him, Kuzava shut the Dodgers down in the eighth and ninth innings; the Yankees had their fourth consecutive Series victory.

Both the Yankees and Dodgers repeated as pennant winners in 1953, and the American Leaguers again won the World Series, this time in six games. Billy Martin was again a Yankee hero, with 12 Series hits. In 1954, the two New York rivals took a year off, allowing the Giants and Indians to win pennants; although underdogs, the Giants swept the World Series. It was merely a breather, however, and the Yankees and Dodgers confronted each other again in the 1955 World Series. Dodgers fans were understandably prepared for the worst, and things did look bad, as the Bronx Bombers won Game One, 6–5, and Game Two, 4–2, both at Yankee Stadium. No team had ever recovered from two opening losses in a seven-game Series.

The Series then moved to Ebbets Field, where the Dodgers, behind the fine pitching of Johnny Podres, beat the Yankees, 8–3. Suddenly inspired, the Bums won Game Four (8–5) and Game Five (5–3) at their home park. Down but not out, the Yankees won Game Six at Yankee Stadium, 5–1. The Series had come down to one game. The Dodgers sent Podres back to the mound, and he pitched a beauty, shutting out the Yankees, 2–0, on five hits. It had not been easy. In the sixth inning, the Yankees had two men on base and no outs when Yogi Berra came to the plate. Dodgers manager Walter Alston had—that very inning—sent Sandy Amoros out to play left field. With the outfield around to the right, the left-handed-hitting Berra lined a pitch down the left-field line. Amoros, who was left-handed, made an outstanding running catch near the line, then turned and fired the ball to Reese, who relayed it to Hodges at first in time to double up Gil McDougald. "That's how it went," the not obviously pleased Red Smith wrote, "because that's how it was meant to go." The Yankees never threatened again, and the Brooklyn Dodgers had their first (and as it turned out only) world championship.

Johnny Podres's teammates fell upon him. As Smith put it, "[H]e was lost from sight in a howling, leaping, pummeling pack that thumped him and thwacked him and tossed him around, hugged him and mauled him and heaved him about until Rocky Marciano, up in a mezzanine box, paled at the violence of their affection." Dodgers fans, indeed baseball fans, will never forget that dramatic game. Near the end of his life (he died in 2008), Podres explained why.

> One thing you have to keep in mind is what happened that day can never happen again. There will be other great seventh games, already have been. Someday someone . . . will make another unassisted triple play, someone will hit another home run to win it all in extra innings. But the Brooklyn Dodgers will never win another championship. They are gone. The events of that day are frozen forever.

The Yankees and Dodgers met yet again in the 1956 World Series, but this time it was a Yankees pitcher who gained the headlines and, in fact, achieved baseball immortality. He was Don Larsen, an inconsistent hurler with chronic control problems, who had, however, finished the regular season with four straight victories. The Series stood at two games apiece when Casey Stengel sent Larsen to the mound. It was a gamble because the tall right-hander had lasted only one and two-thirds innings in Game Two, a consequence of issuing passes to four of the first nine batters he faced. On that day, the no-wind-up delivery he had begun to use did nothing to improve his control. In Game Five, however, it blessed him with a miraculous ability to put the ball exactly where Yogi Berra wanted it. Of the 97 pitches he threw that afternoon, 70 were strikes. When it was over, Larsen had pitched the only perfect game in World Series history—27 batters up, 27 down. No Dodger reached first base safely.

To be sure, Larsen had to dodge a couple of bullets. When, Red wrote, he "didn't take care of the hitters, his playmates did. A savage line drive by Jackie Robinson, a bitter ground ball hit by Junior Gilliam, a long fly by Gil Hodges, all became putouts." As the game progressed, the pressure mounted. As Larsen walked to the mound for the ninth inning, fans in Yankee Stadium—and throughout the United States— held their breath. The first batter, Carl Furillo, flied out to Hank Bauer in right; the second batter, Roy Campanella, grounded out. Pitcher Sal Maglie was up next, but in his stead, manager Walter Alston sent to the plate Dale Mitchell, who rarely struck out. Mitchell took Larsen's first offering for a ball. Umpire Babe Pinelli called the next pitch a strike. Mitchell swung and missed the third pitch, then fouled one off. Larsen then uncorked a fastball. Mitchell started to swing, tried to hold up, and heard Pinelli yell, "strike three!"

Smith's account of Larsen's perfection was straightforward and strangely muted. His account of the Giants and Dodgers' decision to leave New York for the West Coast was, however, anything but. "The departure of the Giants and Dodgers from New York," he declared in a column dated October 15, 1957, "is an unrelieved calamity, a grievous loss to the city and to baseball, a shattering blow to the prestige of the National League, an indictment of the men operating the clubs and the men governing the city." For him, baseball would never be the same.

Four days before that piece appeared, Red was obliged to publish a piece on the Milwaukee Braves' victory over the Yankees in the 1957 World Series. Things began well enough for the world champions. Behind the pitching of Whitey Ford, they won Game One in New York, 3–1. In Game Two, however, Lou Burdette (he preferred "Lou" to "Lew" because of his reverence for Lou Gehrig) went the distance, picking up a 4–2 win. The Series then moved to Milwaukee, where in Game Three Don Larsen, working in relief, won a 12–3 decision. Warren Spahn, the losing pitcher in Game One, took a 4–1 lead into the ninth inning of Game Four, only to give up a game-tying homer to Elston Howard. The Yankees scored again in the top of the 10th, but the Braves fought back in their half of the inning. Johnny Logan batted in the tying run ahead of Eddie Mathews's two-run blast off Bob Grim.

Braves manager Fred Haney sent Burdette back to the mound in Game Five, and the fidgety right-hander shut the Yankees out, 1–0, on seven hits. Back at Yankee Stadium, the home team forced a seventh game by winning, 3–2. Spahn was scheduled to face Larsen, but when he came down with the flu, Haney gambled that Burdette could pitch on two days' rest. In one of the great pitching performances of the twentieth century, Lou again shut out the Yankees, 5–0, on seven hits. Although he suggested that Burdette threw spitballs, Smith conceded that he had come close to matching Christy Mathewson's record of three shutouts in the 1905 World Series.

The Braves and Yankees repeated as champions of their respective leagues in 1958, but this time the American Leaguers reclaimed what Smith called "their hereditary title." He did not think they deserved it, "New York won because Milwaukee wouldn't." The Midwestern ballclub led 3–1 in games and still managed to lose the Series. Game Seven, played in Milwaukee, was tied at two going into the eighth inning. Burdette, who won Game Two, was tiring but retired the first two

Yankee batters. After Yogi Berra doubled, however, Elston Howard singled home the lead run. Andy Carey followed with an infield hit, and Bill Skowron smashed a three-run homer. The score was Yankees 6, Braves 2, and that is how it ended. Lou Burdette did not wait to see the game's final out; "he had retired quietly after the eighth inning, without a handclap in his honor."

The 1958 championship was the last of the seven that Casey Stengel's Yankees won. In 1959, 40 years after the Black Sox scandal, the "Go-Go" Chicago White Sox won the American League pennant, finishing 15 games ahead of the Yankees; they went on to lose the World Series to the Los Angeles Dodgers, four games to two. The "Old Professor's" Yankee squad won its 10th pennant in 1960, and faced the Pittsburgh Pirates in the World Series. The teams split the first six games and prepared for the deciding game at Pittsburgh's Forbes Field.

In his report of the game, Smith informed his readers that Stengel "sent his nonalcoholic, denicotinized, clean-living, right thinking, brave, pure, and reverent right-hander Bob Turley out to pitch against the equally unblemished Latter-Day Saint, Vernon Law, but the lofty moral tone of the duel didn't stay his hand." What he meant was that Stengel lifted Turley after the Pirates scored two runs in the first inning. He did likewise to Bill Stafford, who gave up two more runs in the second. Bobby Shantz then silenced Pirate bats for five innings, while the Yankees scored one in the fifth and four in the sixth to take a 5–4 lead.

The Yankees increased their lead by scoring two runs in the top of the eighth, only to fall behind, 9–7, when the Pirates scored five in their half of the inning. Down but not out, Stengel's boys evened the score in the top of the ninth. The fifth Yankee pitcher, Ralph Terry, who had relieved Jim Coates in the eighth, walked to the mound in the bottom of the ninth. Second baseman Bill Mazeroski led off for the Pirates and took the first pitch from Terry for a ball. "Maz" then ended the game and the Series by blasting Terry's next pitch over the wall in left, more than 400 feet from the plate—a walk-off home run for the ages.

Before a week was out, Stengel held a press conference. "I was told," he said, "that my services would not be desired any longer." In response, Red wrote that, "[T]his was the leave-taking of the most successful manager that ever lived. Thus ended an era in baseball. So closed a glorious chapter in the life of New York." For Yankee owners Dan Topping and Del Webb, he showed no sympathy. "The feeling here is that he [Stengel] had earned the right to call his own play. Nudging him out was sheer effrontery."

The Yankees named Ralph Houk as their new manager, and he continued the Stengel tradition of winning; they won the pennant easily and took only five games to defeat the Cincinnati Reds in the 1961 World Series. But the 1961 season is remembered primarily for other reasons. The American League added two teams and lengthened its regular season from 154 to 162 games (the National League followed suit in 1962). More important, both Mickey Mantle and Roger Maris mounted a serious challenge to Babe Ruth's single-season record of 60 home runs. The Mick was the more likely to break the record, but an infected leg forced him to drop out of the race with 54 round-trippers.

It was Roger Maris, who had joined the Yankees in 1960 and won the MVP Award, who made history. Born Roger Eugene Maras—the family was Croatian—Maris played 12 seasons in the majors. He compiled a respectable but hardly eye-popping batting average of .260, drove in 851 runs, and hit 275 homers; sixty-one of them came in 1961. Precisely because he was not one of the greats, sports writers and "fans" put Maris through hell. As he drew steadily closer to the magical 60th, he earned the enmity not only of those who regarded the Babe's record as sacrosanct, but also those who had rather belatedly warmed to Mantle. Facing constant pressure and a hostility so relentless that it eventually made his hair fall out, the introverted Maris wished only to be left to do his job in peace.

The Yankee outfielder tied Ruth's record in game 159, on September 26. In the final contest of the season, October 1, the Yankees faced the Red Sox and pitcher Tracy Stallard. Could Maris break the record? Would it *be* a record—baseball commissioner Ford Frick, who had been close to Ruth, let it be known that a distinction would be made between records established in 154 games and those set in 162 contests. Maris did not bother to think it over; early in the game, he reached Stallard for number 61. Red Smith did not appear to be enthralled. "Maris," he told his readers, "got 61 home runs where the [Hank] Greenbergs and [Jimmy] Foxxes and [Johnny] Mizes failed because he is a pull hitter who had his best season in a year when all other factors [a longer season, better bat design, a thinning of pitching talent] were in his favor." Perhaps so, but he might at least have added that Maris had been facing far greater pressure than any other record chaser.

Smith could certainly take baseball seriously, and when he did he wrote with serious intent. But reading his work, one is continually struck by, in addition to his command of the English language, his sense of humor. In fact, he often went out of his way to write about the game's screwball side. He found, for example, Cubs owner P. K. Wrigley's bizarre experiment with a College of Coaches in 1961 and 1962 to be irresistible. Wrigley had developed a habit of changing managers at the drop of a hat; he once fired Phil Cavarretta during spring training. Why, he must have asked himself, bother with a manager who would probably not last long anyway? At the close of the 1960 season, he decreed that in the future there would be eight coaches who would take turns as "head coach."

In a piece entitled "The Hot Seat," Red pictured a scene in Wrigley's office in Chicago's Wrigley Building. The chewing-gum magnate sits at the head of a table, around which are vice presidents and several newly appointed "coaches." He explains to his employees that the old policy of hiring a "manager" would no longer be in force, "You coaches down there are going to choose the manager, but we're not going to call him by that title. Smacks of feudalism, in my opinion. We'll call him head coach, perhaps, or chairman of the board." He interrupts his speech with invitations to try various Wrigley gums but finally calls for a secret vote for the first "head coach." There follows, according to Smith, a "pregnant silence . . . in which can be heard faint sounds—heavy breathing, teeth gnawing on pencils, the scratch of labored writing"; and then Wrigley begins to count the votes.

Red must have been delighted with the experiment's results. Under the direction of the college, the 1961 Cubs compiled a 64–90 record, finishing seventh. The following year, they won 59 games and lost 103, the worst record in team history. That was poor enough for ninth place in the expanded league. Fortunately, the freshly minted New York Mets were even worse; they went 40–120.

Even when Smith considered the subject to be of greater moment, he could usually find its humorous side. When, in 1958, he learned that Will Harridge, president of the American League, and Warren Giles, president of the National League, had charged umpires with responsibility for determining whether a pitcher intentionally threw at a batter, he penned a hilarious piece entitled "Pity the Poor Umpire" (originally titled "The Head Hunters" for the *New York Herald Tribune*). An umpire, he argued, "has trouble enough deciding where the pitch goes, let alone why."

An astute follower of the game, Red was well aware that a pitch may simply get away from a hurler. "Is this," he asked rhetorically, "due to faulty control or misanthropy? 'Ball one,' says the believer in man's essential humanity. 'Fifty bucks,' [the proposed fine] says the skeptic. These are the questions that try men's souls." What he meant was that the questions were laughable. He regretted that contemporary players, fans, and writers were more exercised by them than their elders. In earlier days, a hitter went to the plate expecting to be knocked down— it was part of the game. "He got annoyed, of course, and sometimes he resorted to reprisals. But it was not then a tacit rule that a pitcher with shaky control must always be wild low and outside, never high and inside. There is a line so fine as to be almost indistinguishable between the viciously callous and the coldly competent." Wise words from a great sports writer.

"Dying is no big deal," Smith once said. "The least of us will manage that. Living is the trick." Throughout the years, he had occasion to write a great many obituaries for men he had known personally or by reputation. At the urging of Edward Fitzgerald, onetime editor of *Sport* magazine, he agreed to collect some of them in a volume entitled *To Absent Friends from Red Smith*. In the vast majority of cases, he came to praise, not bury, those lost. He wrote, for example, of Joe Louis's dignity and Walter Hagen's style: "Nobody else lit a cigarette with the jaunty insouciance of Walter Hagen; nobody else had his Piping Rock swagger on the first tee; no other golfer walked the fairway with head so high."

In addition to Louis, Red remembered Elston Howard, the first black player to don a Yankee uniform. Howard began his career as a left fielder but soon moved behind the plate. A clutch hitter, he was the American League's MVP in 1963, the first black player to be so honored. Smith noted that Howard helped the Yankees win nine pennants, but he reserved his greatest praise for the man himself: "He was a loyal friend, a polished professional in his job, a cool judge of whisky, and a man of simple honesty. The world will be poorer without him, the Yankees immeasurably poorer."

Red certainly recognized the greatness of Jim Thorpe, whose mother was a descendant of the Sauk and Fox chief Black Hawk. Thorpe had achieved fame as a football player for Pop Warner's Carlisle Indian Industrial School team and as the winner of the pentathlon and decathlon in the 1912 Olympics, held in Stockholm; however, when it was found that he had played professional baseball in 1909 and 1910, he was stripped of his titles and medals. Many, then and now, believe Thorpe was treated unfairly, but Red was not among them; "Jim wasn't an amateur and wasn't entitled to the medals he won."

At the same time, he wrote that Thorpe was the "greatest athlete of his time, maybe the greatest of any time in any land, and he needed no gilded geegaws to prove it." And he pointed out that there was a man in the White House—Thorpe died on March 28, 1953—who retained vivid memories of the "Carlisle Indian." Playing against a "West Point team that included a cadet named Dwight Eisenhower, Jim raced 90 yards to the goal line, but Carlisle was offside. On the next play he went 95, and this one counted."

It happened that many in the sports writer's guild preceded Smith, and of them he wrote with particular admiration and affection. When Grantland Rice died, he wrote of his dear friend and colleague's "limitless generosity, his gentle courtesy, his all-embracing kindness, and . . . his humility." He concluded with a memory of the day, shortly before his death, when Rice and several friends were leaving Toots Shor's. There was some confusion inside the revolving door, and, looking back, one of the group noticed strangers hesitating behind them, uncertain whether they should wait for the way to clear. He heard a woman say, "A lovely man. Let them go." She was referring to Grantland Rice.

We recall that as a cub reporter for the *Milwaukee Sentinel*, Red read Damon Runyon's syndicated columns faithfully. When Runyon died of throat cancer late in 1946, he began his obituary with two wonderful lines: "The waiter in Shor's said, 'That's bad news in your business, eh? About Mr. Runyon?' That was how the word came." It was not unexpected; everyone knew that the famous writer/reporter was terminally ill. But as with any such loss it was sobering, because of its permanence. "To say Damon Runyon's death is a loss to his craft would be like saying breathing under water is inconvenient. Perhaps it should not be said there'll never be another like him. There just never has been up to now." Smith wrote of Runyon's fictional characters, his reportorial skills, and his wit, but above all he admired him as a writer.

"Runyon could do things with the alphabet that made a fellow want to throw his typewriter away and go dig coal for a living."

Smith was never close to John Lardner, the eldest son of Ring Lardner, but he had the greatest respect for his work. Young Lardner, he said, wrote the best lead he had ever read: "Stanley Ketchel [the former middleweight champion] was 24 years old when he was fatally shot in the back by the common-law husband of the lady who was cooking his breakfast." Lardner was a humorist who wrote primarily about sports, regularly for *Newsweek* and occasionally for such magazines as *True* and the *New Yorker*. When he died of a heart attack in March 1960, Red wrote that the loss was "to everyone with a feeling for written English handled with respect and taste and grace."

When, five years later, Frank Graham died, Red experienced a deeply personal loss. For many years, Graham wrote a sports column for the *New York Sun* and, later, the *New York Journal-American*. He traveled on the spring-training and spring-racing circuit with Smith and Grantland Rice, and, when Granny died, with Smith alone (Red doing the driving); they formed a close and enduring friendship. Graham won fame for his remarkable memory (he never took notes) and the conversational dialogue by means of which he brought the human side of sports figures to light.

In the often-anthologized piece entitled "All the Way to the Grave," Graham put his approach on impressive display. In it, he told of the funeral of Joe Gould, the boxing manager best known for representing Jim Braddock. Outside the Riverside Memorial Chapel, those who attended the service share memories of the two men. One of them recalls a day when Braddock was training for the championship bout against Max Baer, or so Graham recalled. After his workout, Braddock is relaxing on the veranda of a house close by a lake; with him are Gould and press agent Francis Albertanti.

The latter hates the country and says, "-------- you Braddock. If it wasn't for you, I wouldn't be here."

Joe laughs and says, "[I]f it wasn't for Braddock you know where we'd be, don't you?"

"On relief," Albertanti says.

"Right," Joe says.

Braddock, we know, beat Baer but lost the title to Joe Louis. He fought one more fight, against Tommy Farr, and won a decision.

In the dressing room after the fight, Gould says to Braddock, "That was great, Jim. And that was all. You'll never fight again. But I don't have to tell you we'll still be together, like we have been."

Was Graham present to hear these conversations? Almost certainly not, but they were consistent with what he knew of the men involved and provided readers with insights into the working relationship and friendship between fighter and manager.

According to Red, his late friend understood his job to be to "take the reader behind the scene where his ticket doesn't admit him—into the dugout and clubhouse, the football locker rooms, the jockeys' quarters, the fighter's dressing room—and let him see what goes on there and hear what is said." So well did Graham do so, Red concluded in his obituary, that he produced the "finest sports column of all time."

Although he admired the boxing pieces written by the *New Yorker*'s A. J. ("Joe") Liebling, Red had little use for him otherwise.

> The fact that he [Liebling] wrote for a magazine deadline and not a daily paper made infuriating reading of the "Wayward Press," another department Joe handled for the *New Yorker*. A working stiff would write a story for deadline, doing an imperfect job, as most of us do most of the time. Weeks later, an omniscient Liebling would pick the story apart, honing his wit with cheap shots. Perhaps he was compensating for his failure as a reporter on dailies.

Red was not alone in his generally low opinion of Liebling. Upon rereading Liebling, Joseph Epstein, who once admired him, found him to be "almost consistently condescending" and lacking in general culture. In his obituary—Liebling died on December 28, 1963—Red did little more than string together several Liebling quotes, and he could not resist describing the recently deceased as the "sometimes salutary, sometimes smart-alecky critic of the 'Wayward Press.'"

Insofar as Westbrook Pegler is remembered at all it is as the scourge of labor racketeers, liberals, and the Roosevelts—Franklin and Eleanor (he referred to her as "La Boca Grande"—"Big Mouth"). And that is not to mention his (losing) battles with employers at Scripps-Howard and William Randolph Hearst's King Features Syndicate. Toward the end of his life, "Peg" wrote for *American Opinion*, the organ of the John Birch Society, but he could not get along with Robert Welch either. From 1919 to 1933, however, Pegler worked the sports beat for the

United Press and the *Chicago Tribune*. An adherent of the "Aw Nuts" school, he was pleased to refer to the Golden Age of Sports as the "Era of Wonderful Nonsense." He possessed, in short, a sharp and irreverent wit.

That wit is on display in a December 1925 piece that Pegler entitled "Siki and Civilization." It was occasioned by the murder of Louis Phal (b. Amadou M'Barick Fall), who boxed under the name "Battling Siki." Born in Senegal, in French West Africa, Siki was the first African to win a world championship; in 1922, he knocked out Georges Carpentier to capture the light heavyweight crown. Six months later, he lost the title to Mike McTigue, an Irishman, on St. Patrick's Day. On December 15, 1925, Siki was found dead on West 41st Street in "Hell's Kitchen." He had two gunshot wounds in his back.

This was a story that Pegler could not resist. Siki, he wrote, "had come all the way from the jungle to the haunts of civilization and chivalry to be shot in the back." He died a confused man. He had learned that it was against the rules of civilization to kill people but "was given a gun with a knife on the end of it and invited to kill everyone he saw wearing a certain uniform." (Siki had served in the 8th Colonial Infantry Regiment of the French Army during the Great War and won the Croix de Guerre and the Médaille Militaire for heroism.) Siki also learned that it was against the law to drink liquor, only to find "civilized men everywhere, white and black, who would sell him liquor and get him stewed contrary to the statutes." When he fought in the ring and blood showed, the "civilized crowds came up from their chairs, roaring approbation." Pegler concluded that "Siki frankly didn't get the plot of this business called civilization."

When Pegler died on June 24, 1969, Red observed that most of the obituaries made only passing mention of his years as a sports writer but that "he will be remembered here warmly as one of the finest sports writers who ever lived." That was a kind and generous assessment from a fellow writer whose political views, although never very pronounced until the last years of his life, were liberal.

Red's assessment of Jimmy Cannon was less generous. Born in New York City, Cannon wrote for a series of New York newspapers. His special interest was boxing, and he forged a close friendship with Joe Louis, whom he described as a "symbol and a force for good, and . . . a decent man." He was also on friendly terms with Hemingway, who was nevertheless often critical of his style. Cannon, he once said, "is going to leave writing dead on the floor." Smith and Cannon often shared a table at Toots Shor's, but Red judged his fellow writer to be insecure, and as Smith's biographer, Ira Berkow, points out, he was particularly annoyed by a column in which Cannon described fishing, Smith's great love, as "cruelty disguised as a sport! Fishing is the vice of the shirker and the rummy." Nor was that all. Cannon went on to say that he had "done a little research with waitresses, bellhops, and bartenders. The waitresses say fishermen abuse them most and tip with a miser's caution."

In response, Red observed that, "Mr. Izaak Walton mentioned a Sir George Hastings, 'an excellent angler, and now with God.' This is documentary evidence of what happens to fishermen when they die. Does Mr. Cannon hope to do better?" When Cannon died in December 1973, Red wrote an obituary in which he cited criticisms of the deceased's work by Hemingway and Frank Graham. When Cannon asked the latter what he thought of his work, Graham was said to have replied, "Jimmy, you remind me of a young left-handed pitcher with all the speed in the world and no control." It is telling that Smith combined his obit for Cannon with one for Count Fleet, the thoroughbred racehorse who won the Triple Crown in 1943.

By the time of Jimmy Cannon's death, Red Smith had joined the *New York Times*. The *New York Herald Tribune* had ceased publication in 1966, and its successor, the *New York World Journal Tribune*, died the following year. Smith carried on as a freelance writer until moving to the *Times* in 1971. In 1976, he won a Pulitzer Prize "for his commentary on sports in 1975 and for many other years." He continued to write after that, although his health began to fail. "I want to go like Granny Rice did," he often said. "I just want to fall into my typewriter." And so he did on January 15, 1982.

3

THE EMPATHIZER

Shirley Povich

For some 40 years, Shirley Povich, distinguished sports writer for the *Washington Post*, was a professional colleague and close friend of Red Smith. Upon learning of Smith's death, he penned a moving tribute to the man and the writer. "Red Smith died at noon yesterday," Povich began, "and there has to be a sorrow in the land." Although Red preferred to call himself a "working stiff," Povich wrote that he transcended his job as a sports writer; "he raised the sports-writing trade to a literacy and elegance it had not known before." He did so without wearing his erudition on his sleeve and while adding an important element of wit to his prose. Smith liked baseball best, Povich observed, but he had other enthusiasms as well. "It was apparent that horse racing was one of his favorites, that boxing held a fascination for him, and that football was all right. He wouldn't touch basketball or winter sports."

When Grantland Rice died in 1954, Povich wrote another tribute to a friend and colleague in the profession. It was Rice, according to Povich, who first demonstrated "that sports could be written with a talent for writing and that even in the sports pages a writer could dominate the language." The "Tennessee gentleman" held fast to the "Gee Whiz" school of sports writing, all but deifying Dempsey, Ruth, Cobb, Bobby Jones, and Man o' War. But that only meant, Povich insisted, that he "resisted the provocative tone and the groping for cynicism that was to mark the efforts of latter-day syndicate writers who grew up in his shadow and sought by controversy a compensation for their own lack of his talent."

Shirley Povich was born in Bar Harbor, Maine, on July 15, 1905. His parents were Orthodox Jews who had come to the United States from Lithuania; it never occurred to them that the name they gave their son might seem odd to their new countrymen, or at least to some of them. In 1959, Povich received a letter from the publisher of *Who's Who of American Women*. Addressed to "Miss Shirley Povich," it invited him to submit a biography for inclusion in the book; he smiled and threw it away. Several months later, however, the Associated Press informed him that he had been included in the first edition of the volume.

What was even stranger, the published biography had been taken from the Povich biography in *Who's Who in America*, which mentioned his wife and three children. Letters of delight from friends poured in, and Povich appeared on the national quiz show *I've Got a Secret*— stumping the panel. The embarrassed publisher sent an apology, in the hope, no doubt, that he would not be sued. He needn't have worried. Povich wrote back that he enjoyed the experience and added, "[F]or years I have been hearing this is no longer a man's world, and I am glad to be listed officially on the winning side."

During the summers of his youth, the decidedly male Shirley caddied, usually for wealthy golfers, at Bar Harbor's Kebo Valley Golf Club. In 1920, he had the good fortune to caddy for Edward B. McLean, owner of the *Washington Post*, who was so impressed with the young man that he arranged for him to caddy for a friend, U.S. president Warren G. Harding. And that was only the beginning. In late summer 1922, McLean told Povich to see the business manager of the *Post* and tell him the boss wanted him to have a job. At the same time, he was to enroll in Georgetown University Law School; McLean would cover his tuition.

Povich's law-school career was short-lived due to the demands of his newspaper responsibilities—and his love of the work. Although he began as a police reporter and rewrite man, he moved to the sports department of the *Post* in 1924. "I could not," he later recalled in *All These Mornings*, "have been plunged into sports writing in a more exciting year, or era. The Senators were about to win two American League pennants in a row, and in August of that year I saw my byline on a story for the first time."

In 1926, McLean appointed his young charge sports editor. "I jumped at the job," Povich wrote in his autobiography, "and later learned that at 21 I was the youngest sports editor of any metropolitan newspaper in the United States." Acting on his new authority, he awarded himself a column; "This Morning with Shirley Povich" ran from 1926 until his retirement in 1974, interrupted only by his stint as a war correspondent during World War II.

Povich was aware that several professional baseball teams, calling themselves the Nationals, had played in the nation's capital in the late nineteenth century. The first significant Washington team, however, was the Senators, one of the original members of the American League, founded in 1901, to challenge the National League. As Povich pointed out in his team history, *The Washington Senators* (1954), the second major league was the creation of three men: Ban Johnson, an ex-newspaperman; Charles Comiskey, a retired ballplayer; and Clark Calvin Griffith, a former pitcher who was to become the most important figure in the history of Washington baseball.

Washington baseball fans were delighted to have a major-league team, but not so delighted by its performance on the field. In its first year, 1901, the Senators went 61–72 and landed in sixth place. The following year was virtually a repeat of the first—a 61–75 record and a sixth-place finish. From 1903 to 1911, they finished seventh five times and eighth (that is, last) four times. After the abysmal 1904 season (38–113), the owners changed their woeful team's name to the Nationals, in the hope of changing its luck; however, most fans continued to call the team the Senators. Perhaps that is why things remained the same. After the team's last-place finish (42–110) in 1909, baseball writer and humorist Charles Dryden coined a phrase that every baseball fan knows by heart: "Washington—first in war, first in peace, and last in the American League" (a clever play on Henry Lee's eulogy for George Washington: "First in war, first in peace, and first in the hearts of his countrymen").

Better days lay ahead, however, because on August 2, 1907, nineteen-year-old Walter Johnson donned a Senators uniform for the first time. Born in Humboldt, Kansas, on November 6, 1887, that good man would soon establish himself as one of the greatest pitchers in the game's history. His sweeping sidearm delivery deceived even the best hitters. "The first time I faced him," Ty Cobb remembered, "I watched him take that easy windup—and then something went past me that made me flinch. I hardly saw the pitch, but I heard it." Playing for a team that finished either seventh or eighth for several years running, he posted losing records in 1907, 1908, and 1909. But in 1910 and 1911, pitching for seventh-place ballclubs, he went 25–17 and 25–13, respectively.

But help was on the way. Before the 1912 season began, Clark Griffith signed on to manage the Senators. Born in Clear Creek, Missouri, on November 20, 1869, Griffith was a small but wily right-handed pitcher whose cunning on the mound earned him the nickname "Old Fox." He played with three teams in the old American Association before joining the National League's Chicago Colts, for whom he labored eight years (1893–1900). In six of those years, he won more than 20 games and developed a pitch similar to Christy Mathewson's "fade-away," or screwball. An ambitious man, Griffith helped Ban Johnson and Charles Comiskey organize the American League by recruiting National League players. He himself joined the new league as player-manager of the Chicago White Stockings, owned by Comiskey. In the new league's first year of play, 1901, he won 24 games, lost only seven, and led his team to the AL's first pennant.

Griffith's White Stockings dropped to fourth place in 1902; it was his final year in the Windy City. Johnson knew that the American League needed a (winning) team in New York, and he concluded that Griffith was the man for the managing job in the Big Apple. In 1903, Griffith took the reins of the New York Highlanders (formerly the Baltimore Orioles) and guided them to a fourth-place finish. He remained at the helm for another four years, before being fired by owners William Devery and Frank Farrell in the midst of the 1908 season. He caught on as manager (he also played a few games) of the National League Cincinnati Reds from 1909 to 1911, but by then he had decided that more than anything else, he wanted to be a team owner. In 1912, he jumped at the opportunity to manage the Senators and, with every dollar he could lay hands on, purchased a 10 percent interest in the team.

The Senators now had an outstanding baseball man as manager and a great pitcher in Walter Johnson. Johnson's grandson and biographer, Henry Thomas, tells us that a bond developed between the two men that was "part father–son relationship, part mutual professional admiration, and the rest genuine friendship." Together they led the Senators to a 91–61 season, good enough for second place; Johnson won 33 of the 91, while losing only 12 of the 61. It was more of the same during the 1913 season; the Senators went 90–64 and finished second. Walter Johnson had an MVP year to remember; let his grandson give us the numbers:

> He won 36 games and lost only seven, leading the major leagues in wins, winning percentage (.837), earned run average, complete games (29), innings (346), strikeouts (243), and shutouts (11); American League batters averaged a meager .187 against him, and he walked only 38 of them—less than one per nine innings; he had winning streaks of 14, 10, and 7 games; five wins were by 1–0, six by 2–1, 15 by one run, and six by two; he was a perfect 7–0 in relief and an astonishing 20–3 on the road; he batted .261, with a .433 slugging average; he was perfect in the field, handling 103 chances without error.

Johnson continued his dominance from 1914 to 1919, posting 20 or more wins each year, but the team's fortunes waxed and waned. The Senators finished third in 1914 and fourth in 1915, before sinking to seventh in 1916. They rose slightly to fifth in 1917 and third in 1918, but in 1919, they sank back into seventh place; the pennant that Griffith sought continued to elude him. The team's stockholders were thus in a selling mood when Griffith met William M. Richardson, a wealthy Philadelphia grain dealer who agreed to back him if they could buy enough stock to control the ballclub. They could and therefore concluded a deal, forming a partnership that secured mutual rewards for both parties. Richardson made a good bit of money, and Griffith ran the club.

The Old Fox had attained ownership and presidency of the Washington Senators. He stayed on as field manager for the 1920 season, which ended in a disappointing sixth-place finish. "The paradox of the 1920 season," Povich wrote, "was that the sore-armed Walter Johnson delivered the only no-hit game of his career, in a year when he won only eight games [losing 10]. July 1 was the date, Boston the locale, and the Red Sox the victims." In 1921, with the knowledge that he was wearing too many hats, Griffith turned over managing duties to shortstop George McBride, who guided the team to an 80–73 finish, good enough for fourth place. But this was not good enough for Griffith who did not fancy choosing managers who had not played for the Senators; for the 1922 season he appointed outfielder Clyde Milan manager. A fine player, Milan was also Walter Johnson's closest friend.

Under Milan's direction, the Senators dropped to sixth place, and Griffith, in a rare departure from his usual practice, named Donie Bush, who for many years had played for the Detroit Tigers, manager for 1923; he could do no better than a 75–78 record and a fourth-place finish. To the surprise of everyone, including the 27-year-old Senators second baseman himself, Griffith next turned to Stanley (Bucky) Harris; according to Povich, many called the decision "Griffith's Folly." But he had made a wise choice. Everything came together for the young manager and his 1924 team. A rejuvenated Walter Johnson went 23–7 after failing to reach 20 wins the previous four seasons. "Pitching ball when you're young is a pleasure," Johnson said a month before the end of the regular season. "When you're old it's a task, and the task grows harder with every passing year. If I could only be for one short month the pitcher I used to be!"

By what seemed a "magic coincidence," Povich wrote, other veterans also "began to enjoy their best seasons in years." Outfielder Sam Rice hit .334, his best performance since 1920. It was no less than a miracle that he played Major League Baseball at all. In 1912, he had left his wife and two small children at home in Indiana, while he traveled to Illinois for a tryout with a Central Association League team. His wife used the occasion to visit her in-laws' farm in Morocco, Indiana; while there a devastating tornado hit, killing everyone—wife, children, parents, and sisters. Sunk in grief, Rice joined the U.S. Navy; he made his major-league debut as a pitcher with the Senators only in August 1915. He hit so well, however, that he quickly became an everyday player.

First baseman Joe Judge, another veteran, had the second-best year of his career, hitting .324. Future Hall of Fame outfielder Goose Goslin had a banner year; he hit .344, with 12 home runs and 129 RBIs, most in the league. Muddy Ruel gave the club what Povich described as "smooth catching and timely hitting," and Bucky Harris played second base "as if inspired." Starting pitchers Tom Zachary (15–9) and George Mogridge (16–11), together with relief pitcher Firpo Marberry, helped Johnson anchor the Senators staff.

Having begun his career during the Deadball Era, Clark Griffith liked his teams to rely on speed, defense, and good pitching, rather than the long ball—and it was a good thing he did, because Griffith Stadium, where the Senators played their home games, was not a long-ball hitter's park. The field measured 421 feet to dead center, 360 feet to left-center, and 373 feet to right-center. Bucky Harris's boys hit only 22 home runs as a team; Babe Ruth hit 46 for the Yankees. The pennant race was tight to the end, but the Yankees finished two games behind the champion Senators, who prepared to face John McGraw's New York Giants in the World Series.

Washington fans were filled with joy, not only because the Senators were in the Series, but also because Walter Johnson would finally be able to pitch in the Fall Classic. The "boy manager" (Bucky Harris) naturally named Johnson the starter for Game One, played at Griffith Stadium. At the end of regulation play, the score was tied at two, but in the 12th inning the right-hander gave up two runs, and his team could respond only with one; the Giants were up one game to none. The Senators evened the Series by taking Game Two, 4–3, behind the pitching of Zachary and Marberry. Each team used four pitchers in Game Three, played in the Polo Grounds; in a somewhat sloppily played contest, the Giants came out on top, 6–4.

The fourth matchup of the Series, according to Povich, was the "Goose Goslin game. If Walter Johnson was number one in the hearts of Washington fans, Goslin was certainly number two." The Goose went 5-for-5, including a three-run homer, and the Senators prevailed, 7–4. Cheered by the New York fans when he walked to the mound for Game Five, Johnson suffered his second Series loss, 6–2. As they had in Game One and Game Two, President and Mrs. Calvin Coolidge attended Game Six, won by the Senators, 2–1, behind the superb pitching of Tom Zachary.

The president and first lady returned to Griffith Stadium for the seventh and deciding game. The score was knotted at 3–3 at the end of the ninth inning, the inning in which Johnson entered the game in relief. Although he had to work his way out of trouble in the 9th, 11th, and 12th, he gave up no runs and was credited with the victory when the Senators scored in the bottom half of the latter inning. The Senators had won their first and, as it turned out, last World Series.

Seventy years later, Povich looked back on that wondrous Washington season. "The likes of it had never been known before," he wrote in *All Those Mornings*. "This was baseball history. The Washington Senators in a World Series. This is not fiction. It happened in 1924. I was there." Bucky Harris's team got to the Series by wiping out the Yankees' league lead, winning 16 of their last 21 games. "It was Walter Johnson, who, above all others, was seizing the moment. The Legend kept the Senators alive by throwing a 13-game winning streak at the Damn Yankees and their hopes of a fourth-straight pennant." Povich retold the stories of the seven games of the Series and their aftermath. "The city's joy was best expressed," he concluded, "by the enthusiasm of the men on the hook-and-ladder float of the Cherrydale, Va., Fire Department, which flaunted a huge banner that read: 'Let Cherrydale Burn.'"

In 1925, Walter Johnson posted another (and final) 20-win season (20–7), and the Senators repeated as American League champions; their 96–55 record was good enough to better their closest rival, the Philadelphia Athletics, by eight and a half games. They faced the Pittsburgh Pirates in the World Series. Harris gave the ball to Johnson in Game One, played in Pittsburgh, and the "Big Train" (a nickname bestowed upon him by Grantland Rice, who was reminded of an express train by Johnson's size and fastball) pitched a beauty, winning 4–1. The Pirates took the second game, and the Senators won Game Three. Harris sent Johnson back to the mound for Game Four, and the great hurler pitched a 4–0 shutout. The Senators lost the next two games, knotting the Series at 3–3.

It was rainy and cold on October 15, but Commissioner Kenesaw Mountain Landis ordered that Game Seven be played. Although he had strained a leg muscle in Game Four, Johnson returned to the mound for the Senators. He did not pitch well and was not helped by shortstop Roger Peckinpaugh, who committed two costly errors behind him. The Pirates won the game, and hence the Series, 9–7. American League president Ban Johnson criticized Harris for starting Johnson for "sentimental reasons"—to which the Senators' manager replied, "I'd start him again."

Harris's charges dropped to fourth place in 1926, winning 81 and losing 69; Walter Johnson won 15 and lost 16. His final year as a player would be 1927. It was a year in which the Senators posted a respectable record of 85–69, good enough for third place but 25 games behind a

Yankees team widely regarded as the greatest in baseball history. Johnson went 5–6, but on August 2, the 20th anniversary of his major-league debut, 20,000 fans showered him with affection, money, and gifts. He retired after 21 major-league seasons, all of them with the Senators. He had won 417 games, lost 279, and posted an ERA of 2.17. When the 1928 Senators went 75–79, Griffith fired Harris and named the Big Train manager. "No manager," Povich observed, "ever took a job with more well-wishers."

The 1920s were exciting years for Washington baseball fans and Shirley Povich, but money was tight at the *Post* and it was 1927 before he was able to make his first long trip out of Washington—to Chicago for the second Dempsey–Tunney fight. He did not think that the "long count" had deprived Dempsey of a victory he deserved. In his judgment, Tunney could have made it to his feet without the extra five seconds. He "faced in Dempsey a ring-weary slugger with a heart of iron and fists of thunder whose stamina was unequal to the effort and who succumbed to the exactment of time's penalty." In his autobiography, written years later, Povich argued that the long count was, in fact, a blessing in disguise for Dempsey. "He became an instant national favorite, a man wronged, an underdog with whom the guy in shirtsleeves could identify." He added that, "[F]or the record, Tunney never would have stopped Dempsey in his prime. At his peak, Dempsey would have licked anybody of that day or any other day."

As the 1920s gave way to the 1930s, Povich continued to hope for a pennant from the Walter Johnson-led Senators. After a poor showing in 1929 (71–81, fifth place), the team posted winning seasons. They finished second in 1930, eight games off the Athletics' pace. Although they did no better than third place in 1931 and 1932, they had winning records. Nonetheless, this was not good enough for Povich, for whom the memory of 1924 was still very much alive. He obtained some consolation, however, when he met Moe Berg, the Jewish catcher whom Clark Griffith signed in the spring of 1932. Berg had played previously for the Robins (later Dodgers), White Sox, and Indians but demonstrated little ability at the plate.

But it was not Berg's hitting or the fact that he was Jewish that caught Povich's attention; it was the catcher's rare intelligence. In 1923, Berg had graduated from Princeton University magna cum laude, with a major in modern languages. He studied seven of them: Latin, Greek,

French, Spanish, Italian, German, and Sanskrit. He also found time to enroll in or attend lectures in mathematics, philosophy, and biology. After completing his first year in the majors (1923), he sailed to Paris and enrolled in classes at the Sorbonne. In 1926, he began studying law at Columbia University, receiving his LL.B. in 1930. After Povich met this atypical player, he wrote without exaggeration that the "average mental capacity of the Washington ballclub was hiked several degrees with the acquisition of the eminent Mr. Moe Berg."

Years later, in an interview with Berg's biographer, Nicholas Dawid-off, Povich spoke of that extraordinary man. "I was fascinated by him, respected him, admired him. He had a great attraction for writers. He brought up subjects that were always interesting." Moreover, in 1932, he had a rather good season. After starting catcher Roy Spencer injured his knee, Berg took his place. He played in 75 games, and although he hit only .236, his work behind the plate made him a valuable member of the team; at least manager Walter Johnson thought so. "I would say," Johnson commented, "that, barring Bill Dickey and Mickey Cochrane, Berg has caught as well as any man in the American League."

Clark Griffith was also satisfied with Berg's play, but not Johnson's managing. At the end of the 1932 season, he fired his longtime favorite and turned to someone who reminded him of Bucky Harris. That man was shortstop Joe Cronin, who was then 26 years old. Cronin had come to the Senators from Pittsburgh in 1928; always a sure-handed player at short, he had developed into a .300 hitter. According to Povich, "Washington fans were completely taken with him."

This was even more so when Cronin guided the team to the 1933 American League pennant, the last the Senators would ever win. They faced the excellent New York Giants, managed by Bill Terry, in the World Series, winning Game Three behind the fine pitching of Earl Whitehill but losing Games One, Two, Four, and Five; three of the four losses were by a margin of one or two runs. In his Series postmortem, Povich wrote that when "they search the records for the hero of the 1933 World Series, there will be no dispute as to his identity. Carl Hubbell will leap out at them from the pages of baseball history." The great left-hander pitched the Giants to victories in Game One and Game Four.

Apparently stunned by their defeat in the Series, the Senators ended 1934 in seventh place, 34 games back of the pennant-winning Detroit

Tigers. Short of cash and disappointed in his team's performance, Clark Griffith sold player-manager Cronin (who was also his nephew by marriage) to the Boston Red Sox for the then-astronomical sum of $250,000. In its own way, the sale symbolized the end of an era in Washington baseball. From then on, the Senators would be known as losers. Povich continued to cover them, of course, but learned to detach himself—"after all," he consoled himself, "it's only a game. Thus, you can have some fun."

In addition to being the year of the Senators' last pennant, 1933 witnessed the auctioning off of the *Washington Post*, Edward McLean having been all but ruined by the stock market crash, his association with the scandal-ridden Harding administration, and his extravagant way of life. The new owner was financial wizard Eugene Meyer, who injected needed money into the struggling newspaper. Nevertheless, staff travel restrictions remained, at least as far as Povich was concerned. He was, however, in Chicago for the Cubs–Yankees World Series game in which Babe Ruth was said to have "called his shot." The truth, Povich wrote in his autobiography, was other than the folk tale. Yankees catcher Bill Dickey told him at the time that Ruth was angry because Cubs pitcher Charlie Root had thrown him a "quick pitch" (that is, before he had a chance to ready himself at the plate). The Bambino, Dickey said, was pointing at Root, not the center-field stands.

Povich was pleased too to have been able to witness the Seabiscuit–War Admiral match race, although he left the writing of the lead story to his friend, the *Post*'s racing reporter, Walter Haight. He limited himself to setting the stage for the race. The appearance of War Admiral brought the crowd to its feet, Povich reported, but Seabiscuit occasioned still greater excitement. There was no doubt that he was the "sentimental if not the betting favorite." Not wishing to reveal the race's result, Povich teased his readers by reporting that, "[O]n the back stretch they [the two horses] presented an unforgettable picture as if horse had been superimposed on horse, swinging into unison and straining for precious inches."

Even more important than the famous match race, Povich was present at Yankee Stadium on July 4, 1939, Lou Gehrig Day. The report he filed that day serves as an example of the most distinguishing mark of his writing and character: his deep well of human sympathy. The first sentences of his piece are as follows: "I saw strong men weep this afternoon, expressionless umpires swallow hard, and emotion pump the hearts and glaze the eyes of 61,000 baseball fans in Yankee Stadium. Yes, and hard-boiled news photographers clicked their shutters with fingers that trembled a bit." He told how Gehrig half turned toward the dugout before returning to the loud speaker to make his profoundly moving speech: "Fans, for the past two weeks you have been reading about the bad break I got. Yet, today I consider myself the luckiest man on the face of this earth."

However limited Povich's ability to cover sporting events outside of Washington, he could, beginning in 1937, report on another local team: the Washington Redskins. George Preston Marshall, owner and president of the Redskins, brought his team to the nation's capital from Boston, its original home. "He struck it rich in Washington," Povich wrote in his autobiography, "gave the fans a winner and provided me with a meal ticket—himself. I punched that meal ticket for years, and he punched back—with everything from trying to get me fired to a libel suit against me for $200,000."

During the war, the Redskins played a charity game, the money to benefit the Army Relief fund for widows and orphans. Povich published an open letter in the *Post*, accusing Marshall of skimming off too much from the profits. But that was not all. He later criticized Marshall for failing to sign a black player until the early 1960s. Naturally, Marshall took offense, and the two men waged a public war until the Redskins owner died in 1969. Nevertheless, Marshall's team, led by Slingin' Sammy Baugh, gave the city a much-welcomed winner in its first year. Baugh had come out of Texas Christian University, where he played baseball and football, and quickly established a strong passing game for the Redskins.

Povich was in Chicago for the 1937 NFL Championship Game between the Redskins and Bears. The first paragraph of his report sums up the action on the field nicely: "In a wild, frenzied battle for points on the frozen turf of Wrigley Field, the deft arm of Slingin' Sammy Baugh prevailed today, and Washington's Redskins emerged as the champions of the National Football League." The final score was Redskins 28, Bears 21.

It was a game to remember and savor, especially because of what happened the next time the Redskins and Bears met in the Championship Game; it was 1940, and the Bears destroyed the Redskins, 73–0. In an interview after the game, Baugh was asked what he thought might have happened had his team's early scoring drive resulted in a touchdown. He replied, "The score would have been 73–7." In providing his account of the game, Povich resisted the temptation to ridicule the Redskins. "Somehow we can't get mad at the Redskins. It was an agonizing experience for those poor fellows."

His sympathetic nature is again on display in the account of an interview with Shoeless Joe Jackson that he wrote a few months later. "I met a poor old rich man yesterday. In his garage he has a Packard and a Buick, and he owns the finest mansion in Greenville, S.C., but he's busted, broke—brokenhearted. He's sick, and he's afraid he's going to die in what for 20 years has been his disgrace." Povich did not challenge Joe's version of his role in the 1919 World Series—the same one the great hitter had offered to others in the long years since; in fact, he cared more about the sadness that surrounded the man than the truth or falsity of his defense.

Two months after the Shoeless Joe interview, Lou Gehrig succumbed to ALS; his death, Povich wrote, "was a sorrow for all of us writers." What was there to say about Gehrig that would not be said by his colleagues? It finally occurred to him that Gehrig was always finishing second. For years he had played in Ruth's shadow, and when, after the Bambino's retirement, he seemed to be in line to be the Yankees' number-one man, Joe DiMaggio appeared on the scene. That was not all. On June 2, 1932, Lou became the first player in modern baseball history to hit four home runs in one game, only to take a back seat to John McGraw's announced retirement from the game. Even when he died, Gehrig's obituary was second to that of Kaiser Wilhelm. Broken in body, Lou was never broken in spirit, and Povich was able to convey to readers something of the greatness of the man, as well as the baseball player.

The 1941 World Series between the Yankees and Dodgers is famous, we recall, because of Game Four, in which Dodgers catcher Mickey Owen dropped a third strike thrown by Hugh Casey to Tommy Henrich. Rather than abuse Owen for the pivotal miscue, Povich chose to express sympathy for Casey. "No pitcher," he wrote, "ever had victory snatched from him in a manner quite as brutal." Povich was aware that other pitchers had suffered cruel defeat, "but somehow Casey's tragic beating this afternoon seems to merit special emphasis in the tragedy department." Povich could not have known, of course, that 10 years later Casey would be at the center of a far greater tragedy; estranged from his wife and named in a paternity suit, he took his own life.

Not long after the World Series ended, the Japanese attacked Pearl Harbor. On that day, December 7, 1941, Povich was at a Redskins–Eagles game. "Unaware of the bombing of Hawaii and war in the Pacific," he wrote the next day, "the bulk of the 27,102 in Griffith Stadium sat through the two-and-a-half-hour-plus game, thrilling to the three touchdown passes of Sammy Baugh." That same day he asked, almost begged, to become a war correspondent—without success. All the more did he envy and admire those like Sam Snead, who enlisted in the U.S. Navy in 1942. The gifted and popular golfer was to serve as an athletic specialist in San Diego, but his straightforward reply to newspapermen who asked him why he was joining up impressed Povich: "Me?" said Snead. "To help win the war."

For three years, Povich persisted in his quest for an assignment in the European Theater. In November 1944, he finally achieved his goal, although the navy assigned him to the Pacific Theater. His first stop was Guam, where he watched a baseball game played by major leaguers. "There's not much doubt," he concluded, "that the two teams out here could pool their talent and win the pennant in either big league." They could boast of Johnny Vander Meer, Virgil Trucks, Johnny Mize, Billy Herman, Pee Wee Reese, and the Senators' Mickey Vernon.

In Guam, Povich boarded a transport plane bound for Iwo Jima. The plane's pilot managed to land on the island while taking heavy mortar fire. On the way down, Povich saw U.S. "bombs drop and then erupt in flashes that gave way to smoky shapes. On the southern tip atop Mount Suribachi, Old Glory was planted proudly." He knew to look for it because photographer Joe Rosenthal had shown him his photograph, *Raising the Flag on Iwo Jima.*

Rosenthal was an Associated Press photographer from Washington, DC. Povich must have known him before the war, and he was proud to write about the photograph. "You've seen it, as who hasn't," he began his piece,

> the thrill-picture of the war thus far; that camera shot with all the beauty of a sculpture piece showing seven U.S. Marines silhouetted

against the Pacific sky as they plant the American Flag on Mount Suribachi's crest. At headquarters here they're calling it the greatest flag picture since Washington crossing the Delaware.

After Iwo Jima and before the Okinawa campaign began, Povich was in Saipan, which was officially secure; however, the 24th Infantry Regiment, comprised of black enlisted men and white officers, had been charged with clearing out remaining pockets of Japanese resistance. Eager to let his readers know that black Americans were among those men fighting for their country—and fighting well—Povich described some of their successful operations in a report dated March 17, 1945.

> Since January 1 this unit of colored troops has killed 185 Japs, captured the same number on Saipan. They go in and blast the Nips out of the jungle with rifle and mortar barrages. They know how to fight in the jungle. They haven't lost a man to the Japs. Only two of them have been wounded.

After leaving Saipan, Povich accompanied the Allied forces invading Okinawa. The invasion began on April 1, and on May 23, Povich reported that the "Okinawa casualties have already exceeded Iwo. At night on Okinawa, you don't move. You lay on your blanket or in your hole and you lie very still, because our sentries shoot anything that moves." He was in the midst of one of the bloodiest battles of the war in the Pacific—against a tough and fanatical enemy. "On shore, the marines and army had to deal with infiltrating Japs, many of them dressed in American uniforms. But on the ships, the navy men had to deal with suicide Jap swimmers, as well as the kamikaze bombers."

Despite having had a share in this hell, Povich always remembered Okinawa with what he called a "touch of fondness," because he was able to share some of Ernie Pyle's last hours. Pyle was the legendary war correspondent who covered the war in Europe before going to the Pacific—at the urging of the Pentagon. He died by enemy fire on Lejima, a small island northwest of Okinawa, on April 18, 1945. According to Povich (and others), he was always convinced that he would not survive the war. In his autobiography, Povich paid a characteristically moving tribute to his friend and colleague. Ernie Pyle was, he wrote, "the GI's pal because he moved among them and shared their living and their gripes and their frights and their heartaches more compassionately than any of the rest of us. He was a great writer—partly because he was a great human being."

Having suffered two fractured vertebrae as a result of being bounced around on military flights, Povich could not join Pyle on Leji- ma, as he had planned. Instead, doctors ordered that he be transferred to a hospital ship bound for Pearl Harbor. From Pearl, he flew home to Washington's National Airport. In typically modest fashion, he wrote that the "reception seemed to fit someone with my war record. There wasn't a brass band in sight." It was summer in Washington, and the baseball season was in full swing, but Povich was not impressed with what he witnessed at Griffith Stadium: "I watched better baseball than this in the Pacific." Perhaps so, but the 1945 Senators posted a record of 87–67 and finished a game and a half behind the pennant-winning Tigers.

In 1943, Clark Griffith had chosen Ossie Bluege, his former third baseman, to replace Bucky Harris as manager; Harris had replaced the departed Joe Cronin in 1935. Bluege was still at the helm in 1946, but the team dropped to fourth place in the final standings, having com- piled a losing record of 76–78. But that was not the worst of it. On December 10, Walter Johnson died of a brain tumor; it was the same day that Damon Runyon, who had called Johnson the "greatest pitcher in the history of baseball," lost his battle with throat cancer. It fell to Shirley Povich to write Johnson's obituary. He recalled for readers, who needed no help in remembering, the Big Train's feats on the mound, but he struck the right note by writing primarily about the man himself. "Here was the man who never argued with an umpire, never cast a frowning look at an error-making teammate, never seemed to presume that it was his right to win, was as unperturbed in defeat."

Anyone who knew, or knew of, Walter Johnson could have written a sympathetic obituary, although not, perhaps, as well as Povich. Not many, however, had expressed sympathy for Johnny Pesky after he held a relay long enough to allow Enos "Country" Slaughter's "Mad Dash" from first to home in the 1946 World Series. We recall, for example, that Red Smith joked that Pesky "stood morosely studying Ford Frick's signature on the ball. . . . At length he turned dreamily . . . and threw in sudden panic."

Povich took a decidedly different and far more sympathetic view of what happened on the play. After reminding readers that Pesky had made a habit of leading the American League in hits, he argued that outfielder Leon Culberson's throw to Pesky, acting as cutoff man, was a lazy lob that misled the shortstop into thinking that Slaughter was pulling up at third. What is more, second baseman Bobby Doerr neglected his responsibility by not yelling a warning to his infield teammate. "So there was Pesky, with misleading information from Culberson and no information at all from Doerr. He wasn't a goat at all. He was a hero for making the play at the plate that close."

Povich always insisted that baseball was the best of games, and as a result, those who complained that it was dull raised his ire. In a delightful piece written in 1975, he told his readers that Red Smith would have been a hero to him had he written nothing more than that "baseball is a dull game only to those with dull minds." It was no accident, he opined, that only baseball had inspired a significant literature. No other sport could "match the deep emotions and substantive human drama in the baseball story." Football hadn't a "single art form to compare with the ballet of baseball's double play at second base with its routine of catch, tag, pivot, relay, and safe landing against 190 pounds of incoming spikes."

Be that as it may, Povich could describe the 1958 NFL Championship Game between the Colts and Giants as an "art form. It had an aspect of Greek tragedy with sudden death the inexorable ticket of one of the antagonists. And it launched a million debates." The Giants had been the better team for most of the contest, but Colts quarterback Johnny Unitas led his team on a late fourth-quarter drive, resulting in a field goal that tied the score at 17. In sudden-death overtime, Colts fullback Alan Ameche plunged one yard across the goal line, and the Colts had a 23–17 victory.

Povich was at a loss to understand the appeal of hockey, "with its overrated violence" and athletes "padded like moon walkers." But basketball was, in his opinion, the worst sport of all. In a famous piece he wrote for *Sports Illustrated* in 1958, he unburdened himself of his contempt for a game that was for "carnival freaks" with "runaway pituitary glands" who stuff baskets "like taxidermists." Then there were the referees, who were always trying to upstage the coaches, themselves a "breed better born for the revival tents. They play to the crowd by kicking up a public fuss at every grievance real or fancied."

Warming to his theme, Povich complained that the rules of the game are "enough to baffle anybody with an orderly mind." He took particular offense at the "one-and-one" foul, about which, however, he was mistaken:

> If the fouled citizen misses his first free throw, he is now entitled to take another, honest [actually, he must make the first free throw]. Failure is rewarded, success in penalized. It is George Orwell's *1984* in action. Black is white, truth is false. Love is hate, and Big Brother Referee is always present.

He concluded by expressing his gratitude for one of America's little-mentioned freedoms—the "freedom to stay away from it."

Baseball may have been the best of games but not as exemplified by the postwar Washington Senators. After Ossie Bluege's team finished a poor seventh in 1947, Griffith replaced him with Joe Kuhel, a former first baseman for the Senators and White Sox. He piloted the team to another seventh-place finish in 1948. Although disappointing, it was better than the cellar finish the following year. His pride wounded, Griffith dismissed Kuhel and recalled Bucky Harris, who had led the Yankees to the 1947 pennant and world championship. Harris remained at the helm for five years, during which time the Senators finished fifth three times, sixth once, and seventh once.

In his final year as manager, 1954, Harris could do no better than 66 wins and 88 losses; his Senators finished in sixth place, 45 games off the pace set by the champion Cleveland Indians. It was during that year that Douglass Wallop—novelist, journalist, and Senators fan—published his second novel, *The Year the Yankees Lost the Pennant*. While the Senators were mired in the second division, Wallop watched the hated Yankees win pennants in 1947, 1949, 1950, 1951, 1952, and 1953. For his novel, he imagined that in 1958, his beloved team would seize the championship from the New Yorkers. They did so because they had outfielder Joe Hardy, a player possessed of demonic talents. Literally.

Young Joe was actually a 50-year-old real estate salesman and devoted Senators fan named Joe Boyd. On July 21, 1958, after the Senators suffer another loss, a Mr. Applegate appears and offers the middle-aged man a chance to become a baseball legend—and lead the Senators to the pennant. It is clear from the outset that Applegate is Mephistopheles and that he is attempting to strike a Faustian bargain—youth and immense baseball talents in exchange for Joe's immortal soul. Applegate agrees to append an escape clause to the "contract," secure in the belief that youth, fame, Senators victories, and the attentions of the beautiful Lola, who is also under contract, will make Hardy forget about his wife Bess and his former life.

Applegate, however, hides a relevant fact from Boyd/Hardy: He is a Yankees fan. At the last moment, he will see to it that the Yankees win another pennant and, most monstrous evil of all, that Joe is traded to the Yankees. Innocent of these diabolical plans, Hardy leads the Senators out of the second division and into a race for first place. He clobbers 48 home runs and maintains an astronomical batting average of .545. In the end, the evil one is foiled. The Senators win the 1958 pennant, and, thanks to Joe's goodness and Lola's true love, our hero is free to return to his wife, even though the deadline to exercise his right to "escape" from the agreement has passed. So much for the novel. In real life, the Yankees won the pennant in 1958. The Senators? They finished last, with a record of 61–93. After finishing last again in 1959, they rose to fifth place in 1960, their final year in Washington; beginning in 1961, they played in Minnesota as the Twins.

Although covering the Senators in the years after World War II was less than rewarding, Povich wrote about baseball events of importance. There was, for example, the breaking of the color line, about which he published a 13-part series, entitled "No More Shutouts," in 1953. "Four hundred and fifty-five years after Columbus eagerly discovered America," he began one piece, "Major League Baseball reluctantly discovered the American Negro." While giving Branch Rickey due credit for bringing Jackie Robinson to the majors, he maintained that Bill Veeck had tried in vain to open the door to black players four years before Rickey signed Robinson. Whether or not that was true—and it probably is— Povich had a high regard for Veeck.

For good reason. Eleven weeks after Robinson made his debut with the Dodgers, Veeck, owner and president of the Cleveland Indians, signed Larry Doby to a contract, breaking the American League color line. A Negro League standout, Doby played in his first major-league game on July 5, 1947. Before the game, player-manager Lou Boudreau introduced him to his new teammates; all but three—and they were soon gone from the Indians—welcomed him. But as Povich observed, he could not stay in the same hotels as his teammates in Chicago, St.

Louis, and Philadelphia. Nervous and overeager on the field, Doby appeared in only 28 more games during the season and hit an anemic .156. In 1948, however, he hit .301, with 14 home runs and 66 runs batted in. He helped lead the Indians to the pennant and a World Series victory over the Boston Braves.

In July of that year, Veeck signed Leroy "Satchel" Paige, a black pitcher 42 years of age. By the time he was finally allowed in the majors, the 6-foot-4 right-hander was already a legend, having been a sensation in the Negro Leagues and on barnstorming tours, including one organized by Bob Feller. In a half-season for the Indians, he won 6, lost 1, and compiled an ERA of 2.48. The following year, he went 4–7, with an ERA of 3.04. That was his last year with the Indians, but he later played three years (1951–1953) for the St. Louis Browns and one game for the Kansas City Athletics in 1965—at 58 years of age. On the basis of his record in the Negro Leagues and his reputation, Paige was inducted into the Hall of Fame in 1971.

By 1951, only four other major-league teams had added black players to their rosters. One of them, the New York Giants, had signed Willie Mays, Monte Irvin, and Hank Thompson. Without those standouts, the Giants would not have been able to keep pace with the 1951 Dodgers, who, in addition to Jackie Robinson, had brought Roy Campanella and Don Newcombe aboard. We recall that the pennant race ended with Bobby Thomson's dramatic ninth-inning home run in game three of the playoffs. Like Red Smith, Povich was present in the press box. "Hollywood's most imaginative writers on an opium jag," he wrote in his game report, "could not have scripted a more improbable windup of the season that started in April and had its finish today in the triumph of Bobby Thomson and the Giants."

Povich knew, of course, that Thomson's "shot heard 'round the world" was uniquely historic, but his account lacked the sense of drama that Red Smith succeeded in conveying. That was not true of the piece he wrote on Don Larsen's perfect World Series game (we recall that Smith's account was strangely muted). He sat for a while after Larsen struck out Dale Mitchell to end the game. "Like any classic achievement," he recalled in his autobiography, "its very excitement represents an instant challenge to the writer being paid to describe it for tomorrow's reader." He met the challenge in his first sentences: "The million-to-one shot came in. Hell froze over. A month of Sundays hit the calendar. Don Larsen today pitched a no-hit, no-run, no-man-reach-first game in a World Series." In characteristic fashion, however, Povich did not forget the Dodgers' losing pitcher. "The tragic victim of it all," he wrote, "was sad Sal Maglie, himself a five-hit pitcher today."

Povich placed a related sympathy on display in a piece he wrote about Roger Maris's run at Babe Ruth's single-season record of 60 home runs. In this, too, he differed from Red Smith, who treated Maris's achievement as all but undeserved. Povich criticized what he called the "prevalence of anti-Maris feeling" and pointed out, as Smith did not, that Ruth was not subject to the same pressures as Maris. The Babe owned the record of 59 home runs; surpass it or not, he still would have held it. Povich went on to praise Maris's conduct, despite the pressure, "His deportment has been that of a guy indicating simply I'm-trying-to-do-my-best." He concluded the piece by calling for greater fairness on the part of the press.

Roger Maris died of cancer on December 14, 1985. Two years before his own death, Povich wrote a moving piece about the man who "left a nation divided between praise and angry resentment." In his view, there had been too much of the latter and not enough of the former. The fans who charged him with lèse-majesté were bad enough, but members of the press corps who insisted he was "undeserving" were worse. They began, Povich recalled, to ask him such personal questions as, "Do you play around when you're on the road?" As a result, Maris stopped talking to them, which only increased their animosity.

Povich was pleased to report that Mickey Mantle, who as a result of an injury had been forced to abandon his own quest for Ruth's record, strongly supported his friend and roommate's chase. He was far less pleased to remind readers that Maris was denied election to the Hall of Fame, an honor he believed the Yankees outfielder, whose clutch hitting belied his modest batting averages, richly deserved.

Although the Maris piece did not quite qualify as an obituary, the Yankees standout having been dead for several years, Povich had many occasions to remember fallen sports figures; it was an important part of his job. In 1961, the year that the M&M boys (Mantle and Maris) were making headlines, Ty Cobb died. In his obituary, Povich argued that it would not do to compare the "Georgia Peach" with Ruth. Each was king in his own era. Ruth dominated his time with power, while Cobb dominated his with speed, daring, and unparalleled knowledge of the game.

Povich did not neglect to mention Cobb's aggressive, almost violent, style of play, but he chose not to dwell on the constant war he waged against enemies (opponents) and his own teammates. In his autobiography, he insisted that Cobb was a "wonderful man in his later years," someone who was generous in his financial support of humanitarian projects and former ballplayers in need. Perhaps he knew of the family tragedy that left a permanent mark on the great ballplayer.

When only 18 years of age and about to advance to the major leagues, Cobb answered a summons to return home, to face an almost unbelievable horror. His father, having learned that his attractive wife had taken a lover, announced that he would be out of town for a few days; armed with a revolver, he returned that night, climbed to the porch roof, and tried to force open the window to the master bedroom, with the expectation, no doubt, that his wife would not be alone. According to her testimony, she heard someone trying to break in, reached for the shotgun in the corner of the room, and emptied both barrels at the shadowy figure outside; one of the blasts blew off her husband's head. In his 70s and dying of cancer, Cobb told the story to writer Al Stump. "I didn't get over that," he said, "I've never gotten over it."

Povich was even gentler in the obituary he wrote for Bill Tilden, the greatest tennis player of the Golden Age, and indeed of the first half of the twentieth century. Tennis ranked with basketball and hockey among Povich's least favorite sports, but he recognized in Tilden an athlete who possessed outstanding abilities. Born to a wealthy Philadelphia family in 1893, Tilden was 27 years old before he began his rise to the top of the tennis world; during the 1920s, he won seven U.S. and three Wimbledon championships, not to mention numerous doubles and mixed-doubles titles. He turned professional in late December 1939, after which time he played mainly exhibitions while doing some writing to continue his free-spending way of life.

Tilden's personal life was, however, tragic. In 1946, California police arrested him for having sexual contact with a 14-year-old boy; he served seven and a half months in jail. Three years later, he was again arrested—for making sexual advances toward a young male; he served 10 months. It was difficult for sports writers to ignore this unhappy story—

although Red Smith managed to do so, writing in his Tilden obituary only "[S]o it ends, the tale of the gifted, flamboyant, combative, melodramatic, gracious, swaggering, unfortunate man whose name must always be a symbol of the most colorful period American sports have known."

In his memoirs, Grantland Rice was purposely vague, saying only that, "[W]hatever Tilden's shortcomings as a member of society, I'm convinced that his abnormal upbringing [he spent his formative years under the guardianship of women] gave him a complex." Povich was not much more specific, "Tilden was not a happy man. He was in and out of jails on morals charges." But he added that the charges against him "would have carried more severe sentences except for judges who were moved more to sympathy than censure and viewed his deviationism as a sickness." Povich clearly shared that sympathy.

If Povich paid little attention to tennis players, he paid even less to female athletes. He did, however, testify to his admiration for Babe Didrikson Zaharias in the obituary he wrote on September 28, 1956. Born Mildred Ella Didriksen (she later changed the spelling of her surname) to Norwegian immigrants on June 26, 1911, she acquired the nickname "Babe" when her mother began to call her "my Bebe." An indifferent student, Babe won early recognition for her remarkable athletic ability. She starred on a basketball team (the Golden Cyclones) made up of employees of the Employers' Casualty Insurance Company, but from the first she preferred individual to team competitions. You get all the credit when you win.

In 1932, Babe represented her company in the Amateur Athletic Union track-and-field championships, winning five (and tying for first in a sixth) of the eight events in which she competed. In the Olympic Games, held in Los Angeles that same year, Babe gained international fame by winning medals in the three events she was allowed to enter: 80m hurdles (gold), javelin (gold), and high jump (silver, as a result of disqualification on her last jump). After watching her compete, Rice, who had met her in the week leading up to the Games, wrote that, "[S]he is beyond all belief until you see her perform. . . . There has never been another in her class—even close to her class."

Three years later, in 1935, Babe took up golf. At the time, there were about a dozen women's amateur tournaments but only one professional tourney—the Women's Western Open. That was a problem for

Babe, because the U.S. Golf Association declared her a professional, as she had been paid a small amount of money playing professional basketball. She did not regain amateur status until 1943.

Playing in the Los Angeles Open, a men's PGA tournament in 1938, Babe was teamed with George Zaharias, a professional wrestler and promoter; before the end of the year, the two married. From then on, Babe was Babe Didrikson Zaharias.

Babe won the 1946 U.S. Women's Amateur and the 1947 British Ladies Amateur, but in 1947, having been named Associated Press Female Athlete of the Year for the third consecutive year, she rejoined the professional ranks. The following year, she won the U.S. Women's Open and, in 1949, helped found and promote by her play the Ladies Professional Golf Association (LPGA). In February 1950, the Associated Press announced that she had won its award as the best female athlete of the first half of the twentieth century. That year, Babe completed a Grand Slam, winning all three of the women's majors of the era: the U.S. Women's Open, the Titleholder's Championship, and the Women's Western Open.

In 1953, Babe was diagnosed with rectal and colon cancer and underwent surgery. Refusing to give up the game she loved, she played in and won the Serbin Open (named after Lew Serbin, president of a clothing company) in February 1954. But the cancer soon recurred. Still determined, Babe played in and won the Peach Blossom Open at the Spartanburg Country Club in Spartanburg, South Carolina. It was her final tournament; she died on September 27, 1956.

In his obituary, Povich described Babe as the greatest of all women athletes, but he added, not by way of criticism that, "[S]he won her fans with her frolic, as well as with her skills." There was the time when, on stage with Hildegarde, the famous cabaret singer, she was asked how she, a woman, could hit the ball so far. Babe's answer: "Just take off your girdle and swing." Another time she helped her male partner win a match with a two-iron shot that landed next to the pin, whereupon she turned to the gallery and asked, "How'd I do?" Povich concluded, "She was so wonderful."

In 1953, the Golf Writers Association of America created the Ben Hogan Award to honor an athlete who continued to be active despite a physical handicap or serious illness. The first honoree was Babe Didrikson Zaharias. The name of the award was well chosen in view of the fact that Hogan himself had made a miraculous comeback after sustaining serious, indeed life-threatening, injuries in an automobile accident.

William Ben Hogan was born in Texas in 1912. When he was nine years old, his father shot himself to death in the family home; young Ben was in the home at the time and may even have witnessed the elder Hogan's suicide. We may believe that the event contributed significantly to the formation of his character. An indifferent student, Hogan failed to graduate from high school and went to work. One of his jobs was to caddy at the nearby Glen Garden Country Club, where Byron Nelson, another future golf great, also caddied. As a result, he fell in love with the game of golf. In 1930, at the age of 18, he announced that he was turning professional. At the time, the professional game was dominated by Walter Hagen and Gene Sarazen, the scion of Sicilian immigrants who had already won three majors—two PGA titles and one U.S. Open.

Despite his almost obsessive dedication to practice, Hogan did not win a tournament until 1940, when he won three in just 10 days: the North and South Open, Greater Greensboro Open, and Asheville Land of the Sky Open. By then he was aware that his principal rivals were his friend Byron Nelson, who had already won the Masters, and Sam Snead, a big hitter from West Virginia. Ben was still in search of his first major tournament win when he enlisted in the U.S. Army Air Corps in March 1943. Stationed in Fort Worth, he attained the rank of second lieutenant and received his discharge in June 1945. The following year, he won the PGA championship and earned a reputation as a big hitter (he was only 5-foot-8 and 135 pounds) and the best ball-striker (someone who consistently connects full in the clubface) in the business.

In 1948, Hogan won his second PGA championship and a few weeks later his first U.S. Open at the Riviera Country Club in Pacific Palisades, near Los Angeles. He was on a roll when, in February 1949, the car in which he and his wife were riding was hit head on by a Greyhound bus attempting to pass a truck in the midst of a ground fog. The moment before impact, Hogan threw his body to the right to shield his wife—and it was a good thing he did, because the steering wheel was driven through the driver's seat. Mrs. Hogan suffered only minor injuries, but her husband was left with a fractured left collarbone, a double ring fracture of the pelvis, a broken left ankle, a broken rib, and deep cuts and contusions around his left eye. There was initial doubt that he would walk again, let alone play golf.

Ben Hogan possessed a strong will and a fighting spirit. Golf was, moreover, his life. In January 1950, less than a year after the accident, he entered the Los Angeles Open at the Riviera. Povich was among the amazed. "The year 1950 has already witnessed its number-one comeback story," he wrote. "Ben Hogan's gallant bid for the Los Angeles Open golf title will probably stand as the peak display of resurgence by any athlete or group of them." He pointed out what was widely known—that Hogan had always lacked the gallery appeal of Snead, Nelson, and Jimmy Demaret. He said little, showed little outward emotion, and appeared to be in his own world; in other words, his concentration was intense. But, Povich continued,

> [E]ven as Jack Dempsey gained wider popularity after his tough break in losing to Tunney on the long count at Chicago, Hogan came into his own after adversity struck him down. Almost unanimously the crowd was pulling for the game little figure of Hogan to take it all at Los Angeles.

And he nearly did. After posting a 73 on the first day, Ben shot three consecutive 69s. His arch rival, Sam Snead, whose reputation as a poor putter was undeserved, needed a birdie putt on the last hole of regulation play to force an 18-hole playoff with Hogan. He sank it. The playoff had to be postponed for a week because of rainy weather and because Bing Crosby's tournament at Pebble Beach was set to begin. When it was finally played, Snead posted a four-stroke victory.

"The Hawk," a nickname Hogan preferred to "Bantam Ben," was undeterred. In June of the same year, he entered the U.S. Open at Merion. In a close competition with Lloyd Mangrum and George Fazio, he came to the 72nd hole needing a par to tie for the title. He hit a beautiful drive and then had a club decision to make; he chose a one-iron and hit what many have considered the greatest clutch shot ever played in the Open. The ball landed on the green, 40 feet from the pin. Hogan two-putted for the tie and went on to a four-stroke victory in the three-man playoff. It was his second Open championship.

But he still had not won the Masters, captured by his old friend (increasingly thought of as a rival rather than a friend) Byron Nelson in 1937. At Augusta in 1951, however, Hogan fired rounds of 70, 72, 70, and 68, and claimed the championship; it was his fifth major title. Two months later, he won his third U.S. Open at Oakland Hills Country Club in Birmingham, Michigan, near Detroit. In 1952, the Hawk won only one tournament, but in 1953, he made history, winning his second Masters and fourth U.S. Open. Wishing to avoid traversing the ocean, he had never played the British Open, but faced with mounting pressure from admirers and his wife, he relented and entered the 1953 field at Carnoustie Golf Links in Scotland. After an opening round of 73, he posted scores of 71, 70, and 68, good enough to win his third major of the year. More than good enough, his 72-hole score of 282 was the best winning total in Open history.

Upon his return to the United States, Hogan was honored with a ticker-tape parade in New York—23 years after the ticker-tape parade for Bobby Jones. On the steps of city hall, Mayor Vincent Impellitteri read a telegram from (golfer) President Dwight D. Eisenhower:

> Millions of Americans would like to participate with the New Yorkers today who are extending their traditional welcome upon your return from your magnificent victory. We are proud of you not only as a great competitor and a master of your craft, but also as an envoy extraordinary in the business of building friendship for America. With best wishes to you and Mrs. Hogan.

Needless to say, it was the peak of Hogan's career. He never won another major championship, although he came close in 1955, when he finished regulation play at the U.S. Open in a tie for the title. His playoff opponent was Jack Fleck, an unknown municipal club pro from Iowa; in one of the greatest upsets in golf history, Fleck won the playoff by three strokes. Hogan was runner-up at the U.S. Open the following year and had top-10 finishes in 1958, 1959, and 1960. He played in the occasional tournament until his official retirement in 1971.

Ben Hogan died on July 25, 1997, at the age of 84. Povich entitled his obituary, "Ben Hogan: Obsessed with Perfection." For good reason. He pointed out that the great golfer "dissected the golf swing. He couldn't wait for sun-up to get out on the course to test his theories. In his hotel rooms, he practiced his swing before full-length mirrors." Of Hogan's reputation for undistracted intensity, Povich repeated with a smile what Jimmy Demaret once said to explode the "myth": "He talks to me on every green. He always says, 'You're away.'"

The Hogan–Snead rivalry was not the last that Povich covered. He was also there at the beginning of the Arnold Palmer–Jack Nicklaus contest for golf supremacy. At the 1962 U.S. Open, played at Oakmont Country Club in Oakmont, Pennsylvania, Nicklaus defeated Palmer in an 18-hole playoff. Although Povich thought it still reasonable to call Palmer the finest golfer in the world, Nicklaus's victory raised doubt in his mind. "Like Man o' War and Babe Ruth, [Palmer] appeared to be one of a generation. Not since Ben Hogan outlasted his fiery rivals, Byron Nelson and Sam Snead, had any golfer been so prevailing. Palmer's kind appeared to be one of an era. But now is it?" As it turned out, of course, it was Nicklaus who became Hogan's true successor.

Povich shared Red Smith's love of boxing. After all, his first major assignment outside of Washington, DC, was the Dempsey–Tunney "long count" fight. On his list of favorite fighters, Rocky Graziano stood at the top. Like Smith, Povich covered the three Graziano–Zale brawls, and, unlike Red, he lived long enough to write Graziano's obituary on May 25, 1990. "For Rocky," he wrote, "the early years weren't pretty ones. He stole, he fought, he lied, he was twice sentenced to the reformatory, he was a sixth-grade dropout, a roughneck, well launched toward a violent, wasted life. It is how he turned it around that is the Rocky Graziano story."

And so it was. The turnaround probably began with the courage he displayed in the three brutal middleweight championship bouts with Zale. Rocky lost the first and third matches, but he came back from a terrible beating in the second match to win the championship. "In his own fashion," Povich wrote, "the new champion did pay tribute to his victim after the fight. 'That Zale ain't no slob.'" That was Rocky— honest and to the point. When, after the fight, Povich asked the battered gladiator if he thought he could beat "raging bull," Jake LaMotta (a possible opponent), Rocky replied simply, "I always did in reform school."

After his retirement from the ring, Rocky emerged as a rather lovable public figure, a man who never pretended to be anything other than who he was, a semiliterate dese and doser with a crooked face. Television sponsors brought him a new and different kind of fame. In his later years, he would express his gratitude in words that have become famous: "Somebody up there likes me"—the title of the 1956 film of Rocky's life. Directed by Robert Wise, the film starred Paul Newman, who gave an outstanding performance as Rocky, and Pier Angeli as Rocky's wife Norma. The film begins with Rocky's youthful troubles with the law and ends with his championship victory over Tony Zale.

Povich was almost equally appreciative of the ring performance of the other Rocky—Marciano. He was in the Garden on October 26, 1951, when young Rocky ended Joe Louis's illustrious career in the eighth round of a scheduled 10-round bout. He was in Philadelphia for the September 23, 1952, championship bout between the unbeaten Italian and Jersey Joe Walcott—and witnessed the devastating right by which the challenger claimed the heavyweight crown. "No disputing now," he wrote in his fight report, "Rocky can hit. Harder than Dempsey. Louis, too, I'd say." His reputation, Povich concluded, could only grow. "He's the home-run hitter of the heavyweights, best fitting the popular conception of what a world champion should be."

Dodgers pitcher Sandy Koufax was at least as great on the mound as Marciano was in the ring. The left-hander broke in with Brooklyn in 1955 and moved with the team to Los Angeles in 1958. His record in his first six years was unimpressive, but in 1961, he gained control of his pitches and posted an 18–13 record, with a league-leading 269 strikeouts. He pitched well again in 1962, winning 14 and losing 7. He won the National League MVP Award in 1963, after a season in which he went 25–5, struck out 306 men, and posted an ERA of 1.88. On the strength of his record, manager Walter Alston sent him to the mound against the Yankees in Game One of the World Series. Like everyone else, Povich marveled at his performance.

Not only did Koufax pitch the Dodgers to a 5–2 victory, but he struck out 15 Yankees, a record that stood until Bob Gibson struck out 17 Tigers in the 1968 Series. "Into the World Series opening," Povich wrote in his game report, "Koufax had taken his glittering 25–5 pitching record . . . and, at game's end, this was the item that caused one Yankee to give tongue to the Yankees reaction in the clubhouse. 'I wonder,' he said, 'how come he lost five games this year.'" The Bronx Bombers might well, he concluded, "wonder about their future in this World Series." They did not have long to wonder; the Dodgers went on to sweep them. Koufax pitched again in Game Four, and outdueled Yankee ace Whitey Ford for the second time; this time the final score was 2–1. The only Yankee run came on a home run by Mickey Mantle, who, because of an injury, had been able to play in only 65 games during the regular season.

Mantle played the last game of his amazing career on September 28, 1968. He died of cancer on August 13, 1995, two months after receiving a liver transplant. Long years of alcoholism had destroyed his liver, and his family. In the last year of his life, baseball's greatest "natural" spoke of his drinking with remorse, blaming no one but himself. As a friend, as well as a sports writer, Shirley Povich wrote a moving rebuke to the dying Hall of Famer's many critics. It was one of the finest things he ever wrote, not least because it put his compassion—his most recognizable characteristic as a writer—on full display. "The stories," Povich began his piece, "haven't been fair to Mickey Mantle. Here the poor guy is, in deep crisis in a Dallas hospital . . . and what is being said about him?" That he was one of the biggest baseball drunks of all time, that he was not always kind to kids, including his own, and that he destroyed his marriage.

Povich pointed out that Mantle "denied none of this in a full confession of his career weaknesses and misbehavior in a *Sports Illustrated* article." Why then return again and again to his admitted sins? Why blame him for the doctors' decision, given the gravity of his condition, to move him to the head of the waiting list for a liver transplant? Where was the appreciation of his legendary feats on the diamond? Why did it not occur to his critics to say that for 18 years he played hurt? In great pain. As a high school boy, Mantle sustained a football injury that led to the development of osteomyelitis, the bone disease that handicapped him for the rest of his life. Povich mentioned this and the serious knee injury Mantle sustained in the 1951 World Series. He went on to list numerous other injuries. "Didn't some of this," Shirley pleaded, "deserve mention in the hour of Mantle's desperation to stay alive, ahead of all the carping about his longtime battle with the bottle?"

Povich reminded those who seemed to need reminding of Mantle's speed and superior play in center field—epitomized by the sensational catch he made of a Gil Hodges line drive that saved Don Larsen's perfect game. And then there was the power. In addition to the 536 home runs Mantle hit during the regular season, he added 18 more in World Series play. No one could forget the mammoth shot he hit off of Chuck Stobbs in Griffith Stadium in 1954—the famous "tape-measure" homer.

Povich knew of Mantle's weaknesses, but he also testified to the better angels of his nature. He was shy, rather than disagreeable, and modest concerning his athletic gifts. When, at the close of the 1956 season, Mantle observed that someone would probably break Ruth's single-season home-run record, he quickly added, "but not by me." Povich wrote at the time, "Mickey Mantle's modesty is unquestionably one of his charms." Why could his critics not write "about his magnanimity toward teammate Roger Maris, when, in 1961, they were both trying to break Babe Ruth's record? When he fell behind Maris it was Mantle who led the cheers for his teammate."

Povich ended his piece with a series of questions for Mantle's critics in the press: "Whatever happened to sentiments and judgments in our business? How did we get trapped in that mentality of the checkout racks? When are they going to call off the dogs? It's time."

Povich continued to write for the *Post* after his formal retirement in 1974, but his best pieces were about sport's earlier days. There were, inevitably, obituaries—for Red Smith, Bill Veeck, Hank Greenberg, Rocky Graziano, Ben Hogan. But there were also reflections on change in sport. In the summer of 1991, he wrote a piece entitled "No Mistaking These Guys for Cy Young." Young pitched for five teams from 1890 to 1911; his total of 511 wins has never been matched. But Povich was even more interested in the fact that he completed 749 of the 815 games he started—54 of them in succession. "The Cy Young Award," he began, "designed to honor pitching excellence in his image, is being profaned every year by guys with seemingly little understanding that baseball is a nine-inning game."

Young would not, Shirley pointed out, have understood how much the modern game had changed. Relief pitchers, once regarded as minor figures who lacked the ability to start, had achieved prominence. Managers referred to them "as if they were members of several species. They speak of 'short relievers,' and 'long relievers,' and 'middle relievers,' with some types known as 'closers.'" Complete games have become increasingly rare. Managers intend praise when they say this or that pitcher will "give us five good innings." To Povich, this was criticism, not praise; his late friend Walter Johnson, he recalled, completed 531 of his 666 starts.

In March 1994, Povich described changes he witnessed in baseball's spring training; they were not, in his judgment, for the good.

In baseball's earlier and less-monied days, spring training used to be more fun for the writers and everybody else. The informality of rickety old clubhouses, wooden grandstands, and the heavenly absence of TV crews and pompous public relations corpsmen brought players and writers together. They stayed and ate together in the same little hotels, called each other by first names, and were uninhibited by lengthy instructions from PR departments. Today "access" is the buzzword. Yankees players are not approached, they are "accessed."

These were not simply the sentiments and memories of an aging writer. The world of sport had changed greatly since the days when Povich was at the start of his career. Baseball was always a business, of course, but it was also something more, something better. When Roger Kahn wrote his famous book about the Brooklyn Dodgers, he entitled it *The Boys of Summer*. George Will, on the other hand, entitled his book about more contemporary players (and a manager) *Men at Work: The Craft of Baseball*. That is all the difference in the world.

Shirley Povich died of a heart attack on June 4, 1998; he was 92. The day before he had written what proved to be his final column for the *Washington Post*. In it, he took issue with his colleague Tom Boswell's claim that Mark McGwire of the St. Louis Cardinals, then on a home-run rampage, had demonstrated that he was more than the equal of Babe Ruth. "To judge McGwire a better home-run hitter than Ruth at a moment when McGwire is exactly 300 homers short of the Babe's career output is, well, a stretch." Long years of watching the game provided Povich with a wisdom that Boswell seemed to lack. Perhaps, instinctively, he harbored some suspicions about the ease with which McGwire seemed to hit homers, but he did not live long enough to learn that the slugger was one of the game's principal steroid users.

4

THE NOVELIST

W. C. Heinz

Off the coast of France, aboard the USS *Nevada*, W. C. ("Bill") Heinz, a war correspondent for the *New York Sun*, felt the concussions as the battleship, risen from a watery grave at Pearl Harbor, bombarded German positions in preparation for the Normandy invasion. Born on January 11, 1915, in Mount Vernon, New York, Wilfred Charles Heinz graduated from Middlebury College in 1937. In the fall of that year, he began work as a copy boy for the *Sun*, a conservative newspaper best known for the 1897 editorial "Is There a Santa Claus" (or "Yes, Virginia, there is a Santa Claus"). In 1939, he earned promotion to general assignments, covering "everything from push-cart fires on the Lower East Side to political campaigns"—while continuing to hope, one day, to be assigned to the sports beat. Before he could realize that ambition, however, the *Sun* sent him to cover the war in Europe, an assignment that changed his life forever.

Heinz's first important dispatches were those that he filed from the *Nevada*. Despite the nerve-shattering quaking of the ship, the 29-year-old observed that the scene before his eyes "was one of strange beauty as billowing gray smoke formed graceful patterns against the sunset hues." (Even though he was fully aware of war's destructive power, J. Glenn Gray—a combat soldier and philosophy Ph.D.—called such a scene one of the "enduring appeals of battle.") As the invasion of the Old Continent got underway, Heinz remained at his post on the *Neva-*

da, while a famous writer and far more experienced war correspondent was allowed to accompany men descending upon the Normandy beaches.

D-Day found Ernest Hemingway, who was to play an important role in Heinz's life, in an LCVP (landing craft vehicle personnel) designed for amphibious landings. He and the fighting men with him were aiming for Fox Green, one of the 10 code-named stretches along Omaha Beach. As he put it in his dispatch to *Collier's* magazine, "[W]e moved steadily over the gray, white-capped sea toward where, ahead of us, death was being issued in small, intimate, accurately administered packages."

To his regret, Hemingway was not allowed to disembark as the LCVP reached shore; he had to wait another 40 days before he managed to set foot in Normandy. Once on land, he set out for Paris with the 22nd Infantry. Soon he found himself in the company of such correspondents and photographers as A. J. Liebling, Charles Collingwood, and Robert Capa. After a series of adventures shared with Private Archie Pelkey, his motorcycle-sidecar driver, Hemingway arrived in Rambouillet and set up headquarters at the Hôtel du Grand Veneur. There he met Colonel David Bruce of the Office of Strategic Services, whose responsibility it was to ensure French general Philippe Leclerc's triumphal entry into Paris. Together with Raymond "Tubby" Barton's 4th Infantry Division, Leclerc's 2nd French Armored Division did succeed in entering the city.

And so too did Hemingway, who, because of his fame, attracted a good bit of attention. While relaxing at the bar in the Ritz Hotel, for example, he was approached by J. D. Salinger, a Counterintelligence Corps staff sergeant who had begun to establish a reputation as a short-story writer before being drafted in the spring of 1942. Hemingway had read some of Salinger's work, and the two writers conversed for several hours.

Although the Germans surrendered Paris to General Leclerc on August 25, the Allies faced determined opposition as they pressed on toward Germany; what is more, their supply lines were stretched to the breaking point. As a result, their advance stalled in front of the Siegfried Line (*Westwall*), the line of fortifications constructed by the Germans in the late 1930s. After the failure of Operation Market Garden (September 17–25), an attempt to bypass the Siegfried Line by crossing the

Lower Rhine in the Netherlands, the Allies attempted to break through the front at Aachen, Charlemagne's ancient capital. The Battle of Aachen (October 2–21) was fierce, with both sides suffering thousands of casualties. The Allies prevailed, but their advance into Germany was slowed.

"If you want to go to Aachen now," Bill Heinz, now with the U.S. Army, wrote the day after the German surrender, "you can drive in and out at will and there is nothing to stop you, for since Saturday Aachen has been ours." Nevertheless, on Dawson Ridge, the "guys who held the key to the city are still dug in—here in the mud and cold and wet and amid the dead, where they have been for 38 days." The ridge was named for Captain Joseph T. Dawson, whose "one lousy little old G Company" stopped three German divisions from reaching the streets of the city. The men of G Company, those who were still alive, remained on the ridge because the Germans had not abandoned hope of taking it and relieving Aachen.

After the victory at Aachen, U.S. forces moved southeast, their ultimate objective being to reach the Rhine River. First, however, they would have to cross the Rur River, which flows across the plain leading to the Rhine. Two dams controlled the level of the Rur, and the Germans, who held them, could open them and flood the plain; this did not at first occur to the U.S. commanders—Omar Bradley, Courtney Hodges, and Joseph Lawton Collins—who decided to reach the Rur by advancing through the dense Hürtgen Forest (*Hürtgenwald*).

As historian Antony Beevor writes in *Ardennes 1944*, "[N]either the commanders nor the troops had any idea of the horrors that awaited them." By the time Hodges recognized the danger presented by the dams, it was too late to alter his plans—and in the thick forest his advantages in tank, air, and artillery support were nullified. The long and bloody Battle of Hürtgen Forest (September 19, 1944–February 10, 1945) resulted in 33,000 American casualties (9,000 of which were the result of illness or friendly fire); the Germans suffered 28,000 (12,000 of whom died), but they prevailed.

Heinz's dispatch of December 5, 1944, began with a sentence that could have been lifted from a novel: "In the Hürtgen Forest, Germany. The road to the front led straight and muddy brown between the billowing greenery of the broken topless firs, and in the jeeps that were coming back they were bringing the still living." He went on to describe how Lieutenant John B. Littlejohn and three enlisted men located three of the *not* still living and loaded them into jeeps. On the way back, members of the rescue team "talked about the Army–Navy football game. They talked about the chicken they were going to have for dinner and about the weather, and when they got back to the collection point the rain had started." This was the only wartime dispatch Heinz's editors decided not to publish.

Dispatches of this kind were often censored by military officials because they undermined morale. In a report for *Time* magazine, correspondent Bill Walton once described the fate of a dead American lying across a trail. The jeeps and trucks that used the trail had to run over him, and he was there for some time before his body was removed. Hemingway was properly angered by the event, and by the censorship. He liked to think of himself as a soldier and did, in fact, see some combat. Heinz later recalled that when the famous writer was not "helping command" a regiment in the Hürtgen, he was "fathering the rest of us." He referred to those correspondents who regularly gathered at the house Hemingway occupied at the edge of the forest (and where he was visited again by J. D. Salinger, who took part in the battle there). On one occasion Heinz presented the host with a bottle of Scotch, the first—but not the last—moment when the lives of the two men crossed.

Having held the Hürtgen Forest, the Germans launched *Unternehmen Wacht am Rhein* (later, *Herbstnebel*), or what came to be known in the United States as the Battle of the Bulge (December 16, 1944–January 25, 1945). In a piece he wrote for the *Saturday Evening Post* in 1964, Heinz recalled the beginning of a battle unprecedented (on the Western Front) in its savagery:

> Shortly before 6:00 a.m. on December 16, 1944, 17 German divisions, moving through the rain and the fog in the wooded hills of southern Belgium, suddenly struck at four American divisions along an 80-mile front. Here in the mysterious frozen darkness of the Ardennes forests, the Wehrmacht monster turned on its pursuers in one last death struggle.

The Allies were taken by surprise because they did not believe the Germans would undertake a great offensive when they needed to ready themselves for a Red Army onslaught in the east. And, in fact, the Ardennes offensive did leave the Germans far more vulnerable in the east. Hitler was right to believe that the Ardennes sector was thinly held by U.S. troops; he was wrong, however, to think that his forces could succeed in crossing the Meuse River and reaching the strategic port of Antwerp. He greatly underestimated the Allies' (primarily the Americans') stubborn determination to resist.

Among the more unnerving challenges facing the Allies was *Unternehmen Greif* (Operation Griffen), commanded by Waffen-SS officer Otto Skorzeny. German soldiers who spoke English infiltrated Allied lines in a failed attempt to capture and protect one or more of the bridges over the Meuse River. They did, however, achieve some success in spreading fear and confusion. On December 23, the Americans captured three Germans posing as Americans; Heinz covered their execution. Taken to the place where the members of the firing squad were preparing for their grim job, he looked out over the valley below. This is the last thing, he thought, "that the Westphalian [one of the condemned] will ever see. I looked at his long, pale face, and I wondered if he was seeing anything. I knew that someone would think of him presently, as they might be thinking of him now, wondering what he was doing."

Heinz did not want to witness the execution, but it was his job and, in any case, he wanted to study his own reactions. Once again it was the German from Westphalia whose fate moved him the most, not least because he believed the young man's story that he had no idea what he would be ordered to do when he reported to his superiors that he knew English well. When the command to fire was given, he saw the young man "pitch forward, hung by his wrists, bent in the middle, his head down to his knees, his long hair hanging, the whole of him straining at the ropes around his wrists. He's not alive," he said to himself, "he's really dead." He wished, as never quite before, that the war was over and he could return home.

A few days before the capture of Skorzeny's men, the Germans laid siege to the Belgian town of Bastogne, where all seven main roads in the Ardennes highlands converged. In command of the defenders was Brigadier General Anthony McAuliffe, who, on December 22, received a note from General Heinrich Freiherr von Lüttwitz demanding the town's surrender. When the note was read to him, General McAuliffe, half asleep, muttered "nuts." At the recommendation of a member of his staff, he drafted this famous response: "To the German Commander: NUTS! The American Commander." The siege was lifted when General George Patton's Third Army arrived in relief.

Heinz did not cover the battle for Bastogne, but he did report on the U.S. taking of the last remaining bridge over the Rhine at Remagen; as a result, the war ended sooner than it otherwise would have. In his memoir of 1964, he observed in admiration that, "[W]hen the first Americans started across they knew it was wired for demolition. They knew that at any moment the whole bridge could go and take them with it, and they had to run 1,000 feet, 700 of them over water. It was one of the bravest acts of the war." After that, "even the German High Command knew it was over." Similarly, the "fear, suppressed for so long, of not surviving swept the troops themselves, whole units, and we were all of us one as the time wore down slowly to that new morning."

A month later, on April 25, 1945, Heinz was at the Elbe River, near Torgau, Germany, where the U.S. 69th Infantry Division, commanded by Major General Emil Reinhardt, met the Russian 58th Guards Division, commanded by Major General Vladimir Rusakov. Forty years later, in a piece he wrote for *50 Plus*, Heinz recalled his thoughts at the time: "If the two conquering and converging armies, still battling German remnants between them, could just keep from firing into each other's ranks, the German surrender could only follow." And so, a couple of weeks later, it did. Heinz then asked for and received permission from Edmond Bartnett, his boss at the *Sun*, to return home. His wife met him at the door of their home. "I could not begin to tell her, no less write it. There was so much that had finally ended."

As soon as he was able, Bill Heinz returned to the offices of the *Sun*, where executive editor Keats Speed greeted him with praise and awarded him a $1,000 bonus. Nor was that all. Speed informed him with evident pleasure that he had approved his assignment as the number-two man in the Washington, DC, office. Heinz's heart sank. He thanked the famous editor but said that he had always wanted to write sports; covering the war had intensified that ambition. During the war, he explained further, he had started to learn how to write "I want to continue to learn, and writing sports, where men are in contest, if not in conflict, and where you can come to know them, one can grow as a writer better than anywhere else on the paper."

After vacationing during the summer of 1945, Heinz returned, dejectedly, to the *Sun* offices, to be told by Wilbur Wood, sports editor, that Speed had released him to sports. He could scarcely contain his joy. His excitement grew when he was sent to cover the football New York Giants, for whom Marion Pugh then played. A quarterback out of Texas A&M, Pugh had only recently returned from the war, during which he had participated in the Battle of Hürtgen Forest. He was stunned to learn that Heinz had also been there. Heinz recalled a report he wrote about wounded Americans cut off in a cabin in the woods. "I was in that cabin," Pugh said. "That's an odd thing." The experiences the two men shared created a bond between them, the kind that Heinz was always to form with athletes who had taken part in what General Eisenhower called the "crusade in Europe."

Football was not, however, the sport to which Heinz was primarily drawn. Having seen men at war, he had come to believe that boxing was the most existentially meaningful of athletic contests. "I find man revealing himself more completely in fighting than in any other form of expressive endeavor," he once observed. "It's the war all over again, and they license it and sell tickets to it, and people go to see it because, without even realizing it, they see this truth in it." Given his view of the fight game, it is no surprise that Heinz found the Rocky Graziano–Tony Zale wars to be unforgettable. Anyone who witnessed their three contests, he insisted, "saw most of the truth of fighting." After the second fight, Graziano, who emerged victorious, spoke that truth: "I wanted to kill him. I like him, but I wanted to kill him. I wanted to kill him."

For Heinz, Graziano was a source of endless fascination and the subject of a feature he wrote for *Cosmopolitan* in February 1947. In it, he re-created the day of Rocky's first meeting with Zale—held in Yankee Stadium the night of September 27, 1946. It reads more like a short story than a sports report. Heinz recorded conversations to which he could not have been privy but that captured the truth, the essence, of the man and the warrior. In the streets, people yell encouragement. "We've got an undertaker with us," one woman says, "so you don't have to worry and you can hit him as hard as you like." Finally, Graziano enters the baseball visitors' clubhouse and is made ready for combat. "In one of the most brutal fights ever seen in New York, Zale dropped him once, and he dropped Zale once, before, in the sixth round, Zale suddenly, with a right to the body and a left to the head, knocked him out."

On September 14, 1949, Rocky entered the ring against a club fighter by the name of Charley Fusari. In another short-story-like feature for *Cosmopolitan* (December 1949), Heinz wrote of Rocky's wife, Norma Unger, the night of the fight. The piece is as impressive as it is original. Between accounts, partly imagined, of Norma's efforts to compose herself during the fight, Heinz told the story of Rocky's courtship, marriage by a justice of the peace, and first years as a married man. After attending a few fights, Norma had chosen to remain at home with the couple's two children; she hated the atmosphere at fights, and it upset her to see Rocky being battered. "It isn't so much that he wins or loses," she said, "but that he doesn't get hurt." She often went for a long walk, usually with her mother, rather than listen to the radio broadcast of the fight. On this night, she was still outside when a neighbor yelled to her that Rocky had won—and so he had, by TKO in the 10th and final round.

Norma's mother was more nervous than usual the night of the Fusari fight and told her daughter they should have gone to see a movie. "That's what I did for the Bummy Davis fight," Norma said. "I saw half a movie." Rocky and Al "Bummy" Davis met in Madison Square Garden on May 12, 1945. Both men were street fighters, and the match was brutal and short. Davis went down in the first round, Graziano in the second, and Davis again in the third. Seconds after the bell sounded to end round three, Graziano knocked Davis down with a right to the jaw. The referee called an end to the fight early in the fourth round. Davis fought one more bout before being shot and killed while trying, with only his hands, to stop four gunmen who were robbing a bar and grill he had once owned; he was 25 years old.

Al "Bummy" Davis was born Albert Abraham Davidoff in Brownsville, a downscale neighborhood in Brooklyn. At the time of his birth, the neighborhood was predominantly Jewish, but it soon became better known as the headquarters of Murder, Inc., the "enforcement arm" of the National Crime Syndicate organized in 1929 by such luminaries as Meyer Lansky, Johnny Torrio, Lucky Luciano, Al Capone, Bugsy Siegel, Frank Costello, Dutch Schultz, Albert Anastasia, and Louis "Lepke" Buchalter. The last two presided over Murder, Inc. (so named by Herb Feeney of the *New York World Telegram*), which was responsible for hundreds of contract killings.

It was, then, in an atmosphere of violence that young Davidoff came of age, and it is not surprising that he liked to fight. After graduating from high school, he became a professional boxer under the name Al Davis. His mother had called him Vroomeleh (diminutive for Avrun=Abraham), and in Brownsville he was called Vroomy or Bommy; one of his managers, Johnny Attell, changed it to "Bummy" because it sounded tougher. The story of Bummy Davis's brief (successful) career and life fascinated Heinz, who wrote one of his most famous pieces about him: "Brownsville Bum" (*True*, June 1951).

By the time he came to write the piece, Heinz knew that he wanted to make of his writing about sports figures windows through which readers could glimpse the deeper meanings of human existence. To that end, he worked to connect the facts of a given life aesthetically—that is, he drove sports writing in a literary direction, making his accounts read more like short stories than newspaper or magazine pieces. He accomplished this, in part, by means of conversational dialogue that he invented or reproduced from memory but that breathed the spirit of those speaking. In this, he was inspired by the work of Frank Graham, a colleague of his at the *Sun*.

Heinz's superb account of Bummy Davis's ill-fated life was a measure of his success. He began with a paragraph that made readers want to continue:

> It's a funny thing about people. People will hate a guy all his life for what he is, but the minute he dies for it they make him out a hero and they go around saying that maybe he wasn't such a bad guy after all because he sure was willing to go the distance for whatever he believed or whatever he was.

In part because of his birth in a neighborhood associated with gangsters and corruption, fight fans began to style Bummy the "Brownsville Bum" and hope that his ring opponents would give him a beating. Heinz conveyed Bummy's resulting hurt by a story of a dog who ran with him and chased a threatening dog away. "Gee, this dog really likes me," Bummy said in disbelief. "He's really my friend." The fight that started everyone hating Bummy was, as Heinz pointed out, that with Tony Canzoneri. Canzoneri was a popular fighter who had formerly held the featherweight, lightweight, and junior welterweight championships. He was, however, past his prime. Bummy knocked him to the canvas twice in the second round, and referee Arthur Donovan stopped the fight in the third. It was the only time Tony had been knocked out, and those at ringside booed the man responsible.

The fans got a measure of revenge when, on February 23, 1940, Lou Ambers (b. Luigi Giuseppe d'Ambrosio), who had once taken the light-weight championship from Canzoneri, battered Bummy for 10 rounds. Bummy was, of course, upset by the beating he took, but as Heinz wrote, "[T]he hardest part was listening to the crowd and the way they enjoyed it, and the things they shouted at him when he came down out of the ring." But that was as nothing compared to the damage done to his reputation by his first match with Fritzie Zivic (b. Ferdinand Živčić), in the Garden on November 15, 1940. Although it was a nontitle fight, Zivic was the welterweight champion, having won the title from Henry Armstrong the previous month. He was also, thanks in part to lessons he learned from Armstrong, a dirty fighter; he thumbed Bummy in the eyes and rubbed his face with the laces on his gloves. To Bummy's disgust, referee Billy Cavanaugh did nothing more than warn Zivic.

Finally having had enough, Bummy delivered a series of low blows to the champion, and at 2:34 of the second round Cavanaugh disqual-ified him. Suspended from New York boxing for life and fined $2,500, Bummy enlisted in the U.S. Army. The United States had not yet en-tered the war, and the military allowed him to fight a rematch with Zivic on July 2, 1941, provided that his end of the purse be given to the Army Relief Fund. Referee Arthur Donovan awarded Zivic a TKO in the 10th round of a fight scheduled for 12 rounds. Soon after Pearl Harbor, the army released Bummy back into civilian life. To his surprise, he got his license back after Zivic put in a good word for him. His managers then arranged a match against Bob Montgomery (a former lightweight champion)—in the Garden on February 18, 1944. Bummy knocked Montgomery out in 1:03 of the first round.

Bummy should have been in training for a fight against Morris Reif, another talented Jewish boxer, the night he was killed. Heinz finished "Brownsville Bum" on a note of irony: "It was a big funeral Bummy had. . . . The papers had made Bummy a hero, and the newsreels took pictures outside the funeral parlor and at the cemetery. It looked like everybody in Brownsville was there." In Bummy Davis, Heinz had found a perfect subject. Rather like Damon Runyon, he liked to write about outsiders, those who lived on the edges of society; it seemed to him that they revealed to us truths about America, and about ourselves, that we might not otherwise have recognized.

As a quintessential outsider who fought heroically in the country's wars, sometime lightweight champion Lew Jenkins was an irresistible subject for Heinz. Jenkins was born in Milburn, Texas, on December 4, 1916, one of seven children. The family was dirt poor and eked out a living picking cotton. As a teenager, Lew began mixing it up with Mexican kids in the streets of Sweetwater, Texas, and soon joined the T. J. Tidwell carnival, taking on all comers. When the carnival folded in January 1936, he bummed his way to Phoenix to see heavyweight champion Jim Braddock box with his sparring partner. Later that year, he enlisted in the cavalry at Fort Bliss, where he became welterweight champion. After completing his two-year enlistment, he and his new wife went to New York, where he headed for Lou Stillman's famous gym.

Jenkins weighed only 129 pounds, but opponents soon learned that he was a dangerous puncher. He won seven fights in smaller clubs throughout New York before Johnny Attell got him a match with Billy Marquart, the favorite who went down in the third round. After another impressive victory, he got a title match with Lou Ambers, then the lightweight champion. A decided underdog, Jenkins knocked Ambers down four times before referee Billy Cavanaugh stopped the fight at 1:29 of round three. After winning the title, however, Lew's drinking became a major problem; when he faced Ambers again, in the Garden on February 28, 1941, he was drunk, though he recovered in time to score a TKO over the former champion at 2:26 of the seventh round. When he was supposed to be training for a nontitle fight against Freddie Cochrane, Lew crashed his motorcycle. Cochrane had him down five times and won on points. "That," Heinz wrote, "was when they wrote in the papers that Lew was a disgrace to the title he held."

Jenkins then lost 11 of his next 12 matches, including a December 19, 1941, title fight against Sammy Angott. In 1942, he enlisted in the Coast Guard and helped put troops ashore in Italy, Burma, and Normandy. It was shortly after the Normandy invasion that Heinz learned that the former lightweight champion was on a Coast Guard LST (landing ship) tied to the *Nevada*. He stepped from one ship to the other and asked for Jenkins, who told him that he was unhappy with the Coast

Guard because "we don't fight." He said he prayed for another war so that he could be a front-line soldier.

Lew returned to the ring at war's end but was never as good as he had been. He finished his career by winning 22 and losing 13. When the Korean War broke out, he enlisted in the infantry because, according to Heinz, he wanted to share in the misery of the front-line soldier. "He became a great front-line soldier because he came into the world in misery and because, when he was making that money and had a chance to rise above it, he felt like a stranger and was not at home in success— and so he sought his level."

In 1952, while researching a piece on what it takes to be a great combat infantryman, Heinz ran into Major General Robert N. Young, who had recently returned from Korea. The general told him that Jenkins was a "great combat soldier. He's famous up and down the front." Lew won a Silver Star and remained in the army until 1963.

In the next to last fight of his career, staged in Syracuse on March 6, 1950, Jenkins lost a 10-round decision to Carmen Basilio, who had not yet won the welterweight and middleweight titles. After Basilio retired from the ring in 1961, Heinz sought him out because of his rise from humble origins and his ability (and willingness) to absorb punishment in the ring. And something more. Heinz had discovered that the life histories of outstanding athletes could be turned to short-story-like accounts if one conversed at length with those whose careers had come to an end.

A high-school dropout, Basilio was teaching physical education at Le Moyne College in Syracuse when Heinz caught up with him. When Lew Jenkins's name came up, Basilio became agitated. "Lew Jenkins? Every time I pick up something he's knocking the stuff out of me. He says I couldn't fight enough to keep warm. He calls me a bum. What's wrong with him?" Heinz's reply revealed more about him than about either fighter: "I don't know what he's got against you, but he came out of the cotton fields of Texas just like you came out of the onion fields around here, and you two should really like each other."

As a boy, Basilio did work with the rest of the family in the onion fields. It was hard labor, and he lightened the burden by "wish-talk," dreams of a better life. One day, he told Heinz, he stood up in the fields and announced to his father that he had had enough. When his father asked him what he would do, Basilio told him he was going to fight professionally. "Well, then," his father said, "you can expect plenty of lickins." "Sure," the young man replied, "and I'll give plenty too." And so he did. By the time he defeated Jenkins, he had compiled a record of 18–2–2.

Coming off the Jenkins bout, Basilio did not look like a world beater; from March 27, 1950, to August 20, 1952, he won 9, lost 8, and tied 2. But beginning on September 22, 1952, he won seven and tied one, giving him a shot at the welterweight championship held by Cuban-born Kid Gavilan (b. Gerardo González). The fight was held in the War Memorial Auditorium in Syracuse on September 18, 1953. Basilio dropped the champion for a count of nine in the second round but was unable to finish him; Gavilan won a controversial split decision. Still determined to win the title, Basilio won nine and drew two of his next 11 fights, earning a title fight, held in the War Memorial Auditorium on June 10, 1955, against Tony DeMarco. Referee Harry Kessler declared Basilio the winner and new champion by TKO at 1:52 of round 12.

Heinz told Basilio's wife that he remembered the fight and Basilio, in victory, dropping to his knees and making the sign of the cross. Millions of people who watched the fight on TV were moved by the scene. What they had sensed, Heinz wrote, "was all the family hardship that had gone into the making of that moment." Later that same year, Basilio met DeMarco again, in the Boston Garden. The result was almost identical; referee Mel Manning declared Basilio the winner by TKO at 1:54 of the 12th round. In 1956, he lost and then regained his title from Johnny Saxton, who was managed undercover by Frank "Blinky" Palermo, a member of the Philadelphia crime family; Saxton's victory by unanimous decision in the first bout was regarded by many as suspicious.

In the biggest fight of his career, Basilio, while retaining his welter-weight title, met Sugar Ray Robinson, the reigning middleweight champion, in Yankee Stadium on September 23, 1957; the bout was for Robinson's title. It is a classic. Basilio was always the aggressor, moving in against Robinson and delivering punishing body blows. In the 11th round, he almost put Robinson down, but Sugar Ray could take a punch as well as he and survived to win the 12th. The 13th was another hard-fought round, with Basilio having the better of it. When it was over, referee Al Berl scored it for Robinson, while the two judges rightly awarded it to Basilio. Boxing laws at the time required that he relinquish his welterweight title.

In the rematch, held in the Chicago Stadium on March 25, 1958, Robinson regained his title (for the fifth time). It was a courageous fight on the part of Basilio, whose left eye closed in the sixth round. In the early rounds, he carried the fight to Robinson, but later Robinson became the aggressor, delivering punishing blows to Basilio's face and head. By the end, both men were exhausted, the older Robinson more so than Basilio. Referee Frank Sikora gave Basilio a slight edge, but both judges awarded the fight to Robinson—they were right to do so. In an HBO special on Robinson, after both men had retired, Basilio called him an SOB, but he told Heinz that he did not dislike his famous opponent. "What I really believe is he was afraid of me. In that second fight I fought seven rounds with one eye [actually it was nine rounds]. The referee gave me the decision and the two judges voted for him, but I walked to the dressing room and they had to carry him."

Robinson was not Basilio's only worthy opponent. He also fought Hall of Fame welterweight Billy Graham three times. Respected as a skilled boxer rather than a knockout artist, Graham had the distinction of never having been knocked off his feet. In his first bout with Basilio, August 20, 1952, in the Chicago Stadium, Graham put on a masterly display of boxing ability; through 10 rounds he kept Basilio off balance while opening facial cuts with repeated left jabs. And as always, he showed that he could take a punch. The decision in his favor was unanimous. In the second meeting of the two fighters, June 6, 1953, in the War Memorial Stadium, Basilio prevailed by unanimous decision. In the rubber match, July 25, 1953, Graham was held to a draw, although his left jab again rearranged Basilio's features.

Billy Graham was born in New York City on September 9, 1922, and fought his first professional bout against Connie Savoie at St. Nicholas Arena (New York) on April 14, 1941. He was so nervous that he wasted little time; he flattened Savoie in the first round. Fifty-seven fights later, he remained unbeaten. It wasn't until September 11, 1945, that he recorded a loss, a split decision to Tony Pellone. In a rematch held on January 18, 1950, Graham won a split decision. By then, he had reached the top of the welterweight ranks, and on February 10, 1950, he faced Kid Gavilan in the Garden. He worked Gavilan over with left jabs to the face and rights to the body, winning a split decision.

In a rematch in the Garden on November 17, 1950, Gavilan won on a split decision. After the Cuban won the (not universally recognized) welterweight title from Johnny Bratton on May 18, 1951, Graham met him for the championship on August 29, 1951. In one of the most controversial decisions in boxing history, Gavilan retained his title by split decision. Filmed highlights of the fight are indecisive—Gavilan was more aggressive, but Graham landed more solid blows and was never in danger. The fight could well have been fixed, for according to Budd Schulberg, who was covering boxing for *Sports Illustrated*, Gavilan was mob-controlled. In any event, there was no doubt in Bill Heinz's mind: "Billy licked Kid Gavilan for the title in the Garden on August 29, 1951, but he didn't get it. The newspapers said he won it [the Associated Press and the United Press scored it for Graham, but the *New York Times* had it for Gavilan], and the writers called him 'the uncrowned welterweight champion of the world.'" In a final meeting, on October 5, 1952, in Havana, the champion scored a decisive victory.

Like Graham, Gavilan and Basilio are both members of the International Boxing Hall of Fame. And so is Joey Giardello (b. Carmine Orlando Tilelli), whom Graham faced on three occasions. In the first, at Eastern Parkway Arena in Brooklyn on August 4, 1952, Giardello won a controversial split decision that prompted Graham's comanagers, Irving Cohen and Jack Reilly, to file an official complaint. At the hearing, however, Graham withdrew the complaint for fear of appearing to be a "crybaby." The second match, in the Garden on December 19, 1952, was again won by Giardello by split decision; it stirred even greater controversy. Graham believed he had won, and so did Robert K. Christenberry, chairman of the New York State Athletic Commission, and Dr. Clilan B. Powell, one of the two other commissioners. They changed the card of judge Joe Agnello to give Graham the fight. The following February, however, the New York Supreme Court reversed the reversal.

In a piece entitled "Punching Out a Living" that he wrote for *Collier's* on May 2, 1953, Heinz described Graham's preparation for his third fight against Giardello, held in the Garden on March 6. It is a portrait of a professional going about his business. Three weeks before the scheduled fight, Graham heads to a training camp along Greenwood Lake, which straddles the border of New York and New Jersey. Heinz described for readers the world of the camp—the Long Pond

Inn where Graham stays, the other fighters in training, a friendly bar-
tender, a dog who cannot perform tricks. Billy spends the first four days
of camp relaxing before beginning his training routine of road work,
exercise in the gym, and sparring (up to six rounds but no more).

Heinz related the story of Billy's humble beginnings. His father, an
Irishman, ran a candy store, which became a bar after the repeal of
Prohibition. He began fighting in the Catholic Boys' Club and dropped
out of high school after two years. He talks about this with others in the
camp but tries to shake off questions about his previous matches with
Giardello. "Joey's a good fighter. I have nothing against him. It was the
officials who couldn't see it." On the day of the fight, one of his corner-
men drives him back to the city, where, as a result of the televising of
fights, he is recognized in the streets. As he readies himself for the ring,
he is composed. "You are always a little nervous (about fighting your
best fight)," he says, "but never afraid because you know you can handle
anything your opponent can throw at you."

Giardello won the first two rounds, but according to Heinz "by the
middle of the fight it was a pro working on a kid" (Giardello was the
younger of the two by eight years). It was a scheduled 12-rounder, and
toward the end Giardello began to run out of gas; over the years, Billy
liked to say, "You learn pace." In the final rounds, Heinz wrote, the kid
was just in there on heart. Billy won the fight by unanimous decision.
He and his wife celebrate modestly in a bar where fans had gathered. In
a perfect final paragraph, Heinz tells us that the next day Billy and
Irving Cohen pick up his winnings ($9,400). "You take out the dough
for the training camp and pay Whitey [cornerman] and take out the
dough for Irving and Jack, and it leaves you about half. Three weeks
later, if the nose heals all right [it was cut in the fight] and Irving can
make another match, you take off again for camp."

Billy Graham retired in 1955, after 126 fights and with a career
record of 102–15–9. In an afterword to "Punching Out a Living," that
he penned in 1982, Heinz explained why he held the boxer in such high
regard. "I will always remember him as the professional, the honest
workman who, more than the champions with their great gifts, represented the rest of us. That was why I wrote about him." He did not
mention that he had written about a fictionalized Graham in a novel
entitled *The Professional*.

Heinz had been thinking for several years about writing a novel about a boxer. He hesitated only because he was earning his living as a contributor to various magazines, the *Sun* having ceased publication on January 4, 1950. He was obliged to devote most of his time to that work. But in 1956, when *Look* magazine paid him a handsome fee for a two-part piece on jockey Eddie Arcaro, his wife Betty said, "Now you can afford to write your book, so write it." He did so, and in 1958 Harper published it.

Heinz was able to write the book in nine months, not only because he was an experienced writer, but because he already had a subject and a novelistic style—he wanted to write in the manner of Ernest Hemingway. He had, we know, come to know Hemingway during the war, but there was more to it than that. He regarded the famous writer's story *Fifty Grand* (1927) as the best piece of fight fiction ever written. It revolves around a fixed fight and is distinguished by Hemingway's simple-sentence dialogue.

In *The Professional*, Heinz tells the story of Frank Hughes, a writer much like himself who plans to write a magazine piece about what a fighter goes through to train for a fight. He accompanies middleweight Eddie Brown (modeled after Billy Graham) as he prepares for a title bout. Eddie's manager, trainer, and confidant is Doc Carroll, modeled after Jack Hurley. Over the years Heinz had written often and glowingly of the legendary fight promoter, manager, trainer, and cornerman. When Hurley died in 1972, he paid him tribute:

> Of all those I came to know in sports nobody else ever fascinated me as did Jack Hurley. He seemed to me to be a literary character, as if he had stepped out of the pages of a novel, and I put him in one about a prizefighter and his manager. A novel, of course, should be larger than life, but there was no way I could make my Doc Carroll bigger than Jack.

In the novel, Doc has the highest regard for his fighter, whom he refers to as the "Pro." Hughes views Eddie in the same way, which is precisely why he wants to write about him. For Hughes, "professional" fighters were a breed apart, superior to street brawlers, whom too many fight fans prefer to watch. Because he believed black fighters were treated poorly—they often became fighters for want of other opportunities and had difficulty getting fights until they reached the top—

Heinz created a black character, Memphis Kid, a former fighter whom Eddie admires. And so, of course, does Hughes:

> Memphis was never a sensational fighter. He was never a crowd-pleaser, because he knew too much. He never went out to make a show. He went out to get a job done. For the few people who hang around Stillman's he was a pro. The people who go to fights don't know a pro from an amateur.

This is the key moment in the novel because it lays out Heinz's views of boxing and human nature. Based upon his war experiences, as we know, he believed that man is violent by nature. The fight game is important because it is (usually) a less deadly form of combat; it is war by other means. So-called street fighters show us the naked truth about ourselves—witness Graziano's wish, while in the ring, to "kill" Tony Zale. But Memphis Kid and Eddie Brown (and Billy Graham) are not "fighters"; they are boxers. They elevate a brawl into an art, and in that way they demonstrate that, to some extent at least, it is possible to civilize and discipline man's violent nature. They do not go for the "kill," the knockout; they win bouts on points.

Eddie Brown loses the title bout because "just once, he tried too soon for too much" and the champion knocks him to the canvas. For one crucial moment, that is, he forgot that he was a boxer, not a fighter. In the dressing room, Doc explains to Hughes that Eddie tried for too much, "He keeps doing what he's doing, he's got to win it." Hughes replies that "it's the only way you can lose," by which he means when we shake off civilized behavior and revert to our animal nature. Whenever that happens, Hughes/Heinz says, "we all lose. Everybody in this place lost tonight, Doc, but they don't know it."

Toots Shor, a friend of Heinz's, sent of copy of *The Professional* to another friend—Ernest Hemingway. After reading the novel, Hemingway cabled the publisher with his reaction: "*The Professional* is the only good novel I've ever read about a fighter and an excellent first novel in its own right." Heinz was naturally delighted and wrote to thank Hemingway and to tell him that he had received a poor review in *Time* magazine. Hemingway replied, "What I cabled was straight, and you believe it. Critics, mostly, don't know much about it. They can't tell the players without a scorecard."

Norman Rubio was, in Heinz's estimation, another "professional" who never held a title. Born Normando Rubio Correa in Puerto Rico on May 30, 1916, Rubio, a welterweight, compiled a career record of 54–24–8. He had his chances at the big time but lost twice to Sugar Ray Robinson. In the Garden on September 6, 1946, he lost a unanimous decision to a 19-year-old by the name of Bernard Docusen; Heinz was in attendance and always remembered Rubio's ability to field questions in his dressing room after the fight. "When we [writers] wanted an opinion" he wrote 30 years later in *Once They Heard the Cheers*, we "went to Norman Rubio because we knew that this was the opinion of a professional who had won title to it through the pains and the ice bags of many nights." That was one reason why, much to Rubio's surprise, Heinz sought him out so many years later.

There was, however, another, even more important, reason; Rubio had fought in Europe during World War II. He served, he told Heinz, with the 9th Armored. "I was a war correspondent, and I was with you people," Heinz replied. "We captured the bridge at Remagen," said Rubio. "I know," Heinz replied, "I was there." Nor was that all. "I was in the Bulge, too," Rubio said. Heinz: "I probably covered you people then, too, but everything was so disorganized that I can't recall it now." Heinz could not help reflecting that, as he watched Rubio take a licking from Docusen, he had no idea that less than two years before the fighter had been through so much as a soldier. He also remembered what he had written near the war's end about all being as one. He asked Rubio if he missed his fighting days. "Yes," the old pro responded, "to me it was fun training with all the other guys." To which Heinz replied, "Yes, there was a camaraderie. Fighters together were like guys together in the war."

And then there was football—*professional* football. In 1949, *Collier's* published a Heinz short story entitled "Man's Game." Eddie is a college football coach whose team is struggling through another losing season. As a result, his job is in jeopardy. His wife advises him to quit and take a job with a professional team, citing Paul Brown's successful move from Ohio State to the Cleveland Browns. Eddie hesitates to do so, but a meeting with the college president and an important alumnus reminds him that, when it comes to football, they are amateurs whose understanding of the game goes no further than games won and lost.

One of his players, an untalented kid named Benson, is also a poor math student. No one, Eddie points out, blames the math teacher for Benson's lamentable performance in class. The teacher is a professional who can achieve success only to the extent that his students demonstrate some interest and ability. As a professional football coach, Eddie tries to explain, he is limited by the football abilities of the boys who play for him. And they are boys. On the field they may impress those in the stands as gladiators, "but when you see them in the locker room, before they get dressed, when you talk with them, you know they're just a bunch of kids. Football is a man's game."

For the boys too, winning is the name of the game, while for Eddie the manner of playing is paramount. Only a pro, someone who has studied every aspect of football, can understand that. Toward the end of the game upon which Eddie's job hangs, the outcome is still uncertain. His boys have the ball, and Eddie hopes his young quarterback will throw a short third-down pass, not a long one that might be intercepted. In a panic, however, the boy throws a long, wobbly pass that is anyone's ball. By pure luck, one of his boys catches the pass, and his team wins, 13–7. The fans go crazy, the boys are deliriously happy, and the opposing coach congratulates Eddie, who, however, knows the truth; "I was lucky."

In the locker room after the game, the college president and the wealthy alumnus praise Eddie for winning. "Eddie," the president says, "you did it." "You sure did, Eddie," the alumnus shouts. "That was a hell of a pass." Both make it clear that Eddie's job is now secure. At home, Eddie's wife greets him with drinks. He tells her that he saw the president. "I suppose," his wife says, "that he's greatly relieved." "I don't know," Eddie replies, "I quit." Heinz leaves no doubt in readers' minds that Eddie will enter the professional ranks, where he will be able to coach men—professionals.

Heinz placed his preference for the professional game on display in the interview piece on Red Grange he wrote for *True* magazine in November 1958. Of course he recounted the "Galloping Ghost's" exploits as a high-school student in Wheaton and college student at the University of Illinois, but he wanted to remind readers that, more than any other player, Grange focused "attention and approval on the professional game. In 1925, when he signed with the Bears, professional football attracted little notice on the sports pages and few paying customers." In the 10 days after he left college, Grange played five games as a pro and changed all that. Before long, thousands of fans were being turned away from games in which he was to play. For Heinz, it was Grange the professional, rather than Grange the college superstar, who mattered most.

There was no more consummate football professional than Vince Lombardi, legendary coach of the Green Bay Packers. In February 1959, after a 20-year career at St. Cecilia High School (New Jersey), Fordham University, and West Point, Lombardi accepted a position as Packers' head coach. He immediately revived the team's fortunes and, in 1961, led it to a NFL championship, the first of five in seven years. As a result, Red Smith, as general editor of a series of as-told-to sports memoirs, chose Lombardi as the initial subject. And why not? Lombardi had already begun to make his reputation, and, as we recall, Red was born in Green Bay and studied at Notre Dame when Knute Rockne was football coach. No doubt he regarded Lombardi as the reincarnation of Rockne. Bill Heinz certainly did. Lombardi, Heinz wrote in *What a Time It Was*, "inspired and moved people who knew him, or didn't, as none other in his *profession* [italics added] but Knute Rockne a quarter-century before." It is worth noting in that regard that as a college football player at Fordham, Lombardi had been coached by Jim Crowley, one of Rockne's Four Horsemen.

Smith chose his good friend Bill Heinz as the collaborating author for the Lombardi memoir. Lombardi's wife Marie, who had often heard her husband use the expression, gave Heinz his title: *Run to Daylight!* Working with Coach Lombardi, Heinz quickly discovered, was rather like pulling teeth; his memory of details was all but nonexistent, and he resented having to take time away from his profession. Recalling the piece he had written about Rocky Graziano on the day he was to fight Tony Zale, Heinz elected to focus on the week before the Packers' October 1962 game against the Detroit Lions. Whatever he could get out of Lombardi would be supplemented by information from Marie Lombardi and some of the Packers players. It worked, and the resulting book became a sports classic.

On the Monday preceding game day, Lombardi takes a few minutes to describe his views on winning—although of course not in publishable prose; Heinz provided that. "We try," Lombardi tells Heinz, "to make it as uncomplicated as we can, because I believe that if you block and tackle better than the other team and the breaks are even you're going to win." He makes it clear that he prefers the running to the passing game. When he came into the NFL, he was surprised to find that few coaches believed you could sustain a running game against the pros, whose defensive players were too big and too mobile. Moreover, a running play required the split-second timing of at least seven or eight men. Nevertheless, Lombardi remained confident in his and his team's ability to run the ball, "What it comes down to is that to have a good running game you have to like to run as a coach. You have to derive more creative satisfaction from the planning and the polishing of the coordination of seven or eight men rather than two or three [needed for a pass play]."

Lombardi proved to be an astute judge of a player's abilities, and he enjoyed talking about them. He describes defensive end and future Hall of Famer Willie Davis as a "great one. For a big man—6-foot-3 and 240 pounds—he has excellent agility, and he has great sincerity and determination." Right guard Jerry Kramer has the "perfect devil-may-care attitude it takes to play this game." He and left guard Fuzzy Thurston, together with fullback Jim Taylor, block for Paul Hornung in the famous running play known as the "Lombardi Sweep." Middle linebacker Ray Nitschke does not respond to criticism well, but he is a great one. According to Lombardi, Nitschke is a "big, 6-foot-3, 235-pound, rough, belligerent, fun-loving guy with a heart as big as all outdoors." Lombardi describes wide receiver Boyd Dowler as "serious, intense, and highly intelligent"; good at spotting defenses, he is rarely guilty of an error in judgment.

No position player is more important, Lombardi tells Heinz, than the quarterback. That is so because, "if this is a game through which you find self-expression—and if it isn't you don't belong in it—then that quarterback is the primary extension of yourself, and he is your greatest challenge." He is fortunate, therefore, to have for his quarterback Bart Starr, whom he credits with an analytic mind, retentive memory, and inner toughness. He is so good at calling plays that Lombardi rarely sends in more than 10 (of the 65 or 70 the Packers run in the course of a game). Starr possesses a thorough knowledge of what each of his teammates has to do on every play and is able to list the qualities and characteristics of each individual on the opposing team.

In a hard-fought game that is not decided until the final minute of play, the Packers defeat the Lions, 9–7. Lombardi praises his players, especially those who played particularly well. But he can't allow them (including himself) to rest on their laurels. "Let's remember this," he tells them after the game. "We were the better team. We made mistakes, and let's not forget it. Let's stop making mistakes. Have your fun now. You deserve it, but you get down to work again on Tuesday. That's all."

As we have seen, both Red Smith and Shirley Povich disliked hockey. Bill Heinz, on the other hand, saw in it the same (semicontrolled) violent combat that attracted him to boxing and football. From the 1942–1943 season to the 1967–1968 season, the NHL was comprised of the "Original Six" teams: Chicago Black Hawks, Montreal Canadiens, New York Rangers, Toronto Maple Leafs, Boston Bruins, and Detroit Red Wings. During the 1950s, the Red Wings came to dominate the game, largely because of the presence on their roster of Gordie Howe. Regarded then, and now, as the greatest all-round player in the game's history, Howe was born March 31, 1928, in Floral, Saskatchewan, and grew up in nearby Saskatoon.

He broke in with the Red Wings in 1946 at the age of 18, and it was not long before his only rival for preeminence in the game was high-scoring Canadiens right winger Maurice (Rocket) Richard. Quiet and self-effacing off the ice, Howe was a no-holds-barred fighter on it. Teamed on the "Production Line" (front line) with Sid Abel and Ted Lindsay, he led the Red Wings to four Stanley Cup victories in the seven postseasons between 1950 and 1956. Along the way, he won the Art Ross Trophy (NHL leading scorer) in 1951, 1952, 1953, 1954, and 1957, and the Hart Memorial Trophy (NHL most valuable player) in 1952, 1953, 1957, and 1958.

In the January 10, 1959, issue of the *Saturday Evening Post*, Heinz published an admiring piece on Howe. Although he did not fail to call attention to "Mr. Hockey's" remarkable skills, he was more interested in his fierce battles with opponents. Howe's wife Colleen told him that she first heard of her future husband when he nearly lost his life in the first game of the 1950 playoff semifinals against the Toronto Maple Leafs. Enraged by some offense committed by the Leafs' Ted Kennedy, he hurled his body at his enemy. When Kennedy moved out of the way of the charge, Howe plunged headfirst into the boards, the side of his face hitting the wooden molding running along the top edge. He suffered a fractured nose and cheekbone, a lacerated eyeball, and hemorrhaging of the brain. Dr. Frederic Schreiber had to drill a small opening in Howe's skull and drain fluid to relieve pressure on the brain, saving his patient's life.

Heinz recited with obvious awe a partial list of Howe's injuries,

> He has had operations on both knees, and they had to put him under anesthesia to clean a long gash in his left thigh. Six years ago he played 15 games with his broken right wrist in a cast and led the league in goals and assists, while setting an all-time season record of 95 points. Last year his left shoulder was dislocated, and a week later he was hospitalized for 10 days with torn rib cartilages.

Many of Howe's injuries were the result of violent encounters with opposing players, none of which was forgotten. Gus Mortson of Toronto, later a teammate, once took out some of Howe's teeth with a carefully aimed elbow; weeks later, Howe's stick broke Mortson's nose. Later still, Mortson's body check put Howe in the hospital. Hockey, clearly, was Heinz's kind of game.

Of the major sports, baseball was Heinz's least favorite. Nevertheless, there were certain players, active or retired, whom he sought out. One of them was Yankees reserve catcher Ralph Houk. Born in Kansas on August 9, 1919, Houk signed with the Yankees in 1939 and played in the farm system until he joined the U.S. Army on February 22, 1942. He attended armored officers' candidate school, graduated as a second lieutenant, and arrived on the European continent with Company I, 89th Cavalry Reconnaissance Squadron (mechanized) of the 9th Armored Division in September 1944. He distinguished himself during the Battle of the Bulge and at the Remagen Bridge. He left the army as a major and the recipient of a Purple Heart, Silver Star, and Bronze Star.

Houk joined the Yankees in 1947 and remained on the team through the 1954 season. It was his misfortune, however, to play behind Yogi Berra; in his eight seasons as a player, he appeared in only 91 games. Heinz was understandably interested in Houk's war record, and in 1950 he seized an opportunity to meet with him in the Yankees dugout. The conversation soon turned to Remagen, and Houk asked if Heinz remembered a road that turned along the river. "Sure," Heinz replied,

"You know the river's nowhere near as wide there as the Hudson, and I could see and hear a firefight going on over there in the trees just south of the bridge." Houk could scarcely believe his ears. "You saw that?" he exclaimed. "That was me. We had a hell of a firefight there. I'll be damned."

After a few years as a minor-league manager and Yankees coach, Houk succeeded Casey Stengel as Yankees skipper at the end of the 1960 season. He led the team to world championships in 1961 and 1962, and to the American League pennant in 1963. He became general manager at the close of the 1963 season but returned as manager in 1966. During his second tenure (1966–1973), he was unable to lead the team to the pennant. But that did not matter to Heinz; it was Houk the man, not Houk the player or manager, who interested him.

Heinz was always particularly interested in athletes off the field or out of the ring. As a novelist and short-story writer, he wanted to get to know them as people, not simply as performers. He told Carmen Basilio that he had always wondered "if the people who went to the events ever conceived of the athletes as being other than as they then saw them." After all, "fighters didn't come into the world wearing white trunks and eight-ounce gloves." This helps explain why he often wrote about athletes in retirement. He collected a number of his literary interviews with retired athletes in a book entitled *Once They Heard the Cheers* (1979).

He entitled one of the interviews in that volume "The Shy One"—a profile of former heavyweight champion Floyd Patterson. We remember that Patterson, who won the middleweight Olympic gold medal at the 1952 Helsinki Games, claimed the title by defeating Archie Moore in an elimination tournament to determine Rocky Marciano's successor. After four successful defensives against indifferent opponents, he suffered a humiliating defeat at the hands, or rather the right hand, of Ingemar Johansson on June 25, 1959. A year later, however, he regained the crown by knocking the Swedish champion out cold. The two fighters met for a third time on March 13, 1961, with Patterson again the winner.

Patterson defended his title against Tom McNeeley, but on September 25, 1962, mob-connected ex-convict Sonny Liston knocked him out in the first round. The return match of July 22, 1963, was a repeat of the first, with Liston scoring another first-round knockout. Embarrassed and shy by nature, Floyd fought three of his next five fights—all of which he won—in Sweden. These victories earned him another shot at regaining the championship; on November 22, 1965, he met reigning champion Muhammed Ali in Las Vegas. There was no love lost between the two men. Before the fight, Patterson called Ali "Cassius Clay," his name at birth, and said that the "image of a black Muslim as the world heavyweight champion disgraces the sport and the nation."

Taller, heavier, stronger, quicker, and possessed of a longer reach, Ali dominated Patterson from the beginning. In the first round, he danced around, taunted Patterson repeatedly, and never threw a punch. He scored a knockdown in round six and, in the remaining rounds, punished Patterson without knocking him out. Having seen enough, referee Harold Krause stopped the fight at 2:18 of round 12. When it was finally over, Joe Louis put into words what everyone who witnessed the fight knew: "He could have knocked Patterson out whenever he wanted, but let's face it, Clay is selfish and cruel." It would not be the last time Ali taunted and cut up a weaker opponent.

In the final match of his career, fought in the Garden on September 20, 1972, Patterson met Ali for the second time. The result was the same. By the sixth round, Ali, who derived obvious pleasure from humiliating his adversary, had closed Patterson's left eye, and at the end of round seven referee Arthur Mercante refused to allow the fight to continue. Patterson told Bill Heinz that he was once asked to speak to a group of black college students, one of whom asked him why he called Ali Cassius Clay. He wondered, he said in answer, why the students refused to grant him the same right they granted Ali: "I believe Clay believes in a separate society. You believe the same, or you wouldn't be all blacks here. He called Liston 'The Ugly Bear.' He called George Forman 'The Mummy.' He called me 'The Rabbit.' You must give me the right to call him 'Clay.'"

His encounter with the black students was indicative of Patterson's attitude toward racial matters. Today [sometime in the 1970s], he told Heinz, "you must be militant—down with Whitey—to be accepted. . . . I believe in an equal society. I see no colors. Everybody is the same, like in my gym—but the militants don't like me." Perhaps not, but Heinz recognized his strength of character.

He always seemed to me to be the most miscast of fighters, for while
he had the physical attributes to be a great fighter—always excepting
his inability to absorb a heavyweight's big punch—he also had the
compassion of a priest, and I never knew anyone else in sports whose
antennae were so attuned to the suffering of others.

Whereas Heinz found Patterson to be an open book, he failed in his
attempt to gain an understanding of Sugar Ray Robinson as a person.
When, in the early 1950s, Robinson asked him to ghost an autobiography, he declined. "I just can't do it, Ray," he said. "There are those
conflicting versions of those events in your life, in and out of boxing."
Chief among them was Robinson's army record. During the war, he was
a member of the Joe Louis Troupe, which entertained the troops by
fighting exhibitions; however, when the troupe sailed for Europe on
March 31, 1944, Robinson was not aboard. Years later he claimed that,
at the time, he was suffering from amnesia and had been hospitalized.
When Heinz traveled to California in the 1970s to conduct an interview
for *Once They Heard the Cheers*, he told Robinson that that story had
made him less popular than Rocky Graziano, who had been given a
dishonorable discharge; Robinson's discharge was honorable.

The difference, according to Heinz, was that Rocky was "open and
frank, and you're not, really. What I want to do is explain you. . . . If I
understand, I can make the readers understand, and as I said, that can
mean a lot to you, if you'll level with me." Unfortunately, Robinson did
not level. Upon learning that Heinz had been a war correspondent in
Europe, he expressed surprise that their paths had not crossed. "We
were over there," he said with a straight face. "Joe Louis and I, we had a
troupe, and we boxed in the ETO [European Theater of Operations]
and everything." At the conclusion of his piece, therefore, Heinz offered these sad words: "I saw him start up the sidewalk, the greatest
fighter I ever saw, the one I wanted so much to know."

Not all of Heinz's subjects in *Once They Heard the Cheers* were
fighters. He wrote, too, of the "Fireman," former Yankees relief ace Joe
Page. A fireballing left-hander, Page pitched for the Yankees from 1944
to 1950, his best years coming from 1947 to 1950. In 1949, when the
Yankees won the American League pennant and the World Series, Page
pitched in 60 games, winning 13, losing 8, and saving 27; he posted an
ERA of 2.59. It was his finest season. In 1950, he injured his hip throwing and went 3–7, with 13 saves and an ERA of 5.04. The Yankees sent

him to the minors, and he never returned. In 1954, he caught on with the Pirates but pitched in only seven games before being released.

In 1976, Heinz visited Page at Joe Page's Rocky Lodge in Laughlin-town, Pennsylvania. It had been more than 20 years since the Fireman threw his last pitch; his first marriage had ended in divorce, he had a heart attack, and he was suffering from throat cancer. To his traveling companion Skipper Lofting, rodeo press agent and short-story writer, Heinz explained why he wanted to see Page, "That's what's wrong with this business. We're a lot of hustlers. We latch on to someone because he's in the public eye and we need to make a living. . . . Then we say good-bye and good luck, and if his luck runs out where are we? We're long gone, and on to somebody else."

Heinz had learned this from bitter experience. He recalled watching as Page pitched his last game for the Yankees—a game he lost. When the game ended he went down to the clubhouse. Page "always had the dressing stall next to DiMaggio, and he was sitting there with his head down. I said, 'Joe, tough luck.' He looked up at me, and he said, 'Billy, you're jinxin' me.'" He referred to Heinz's *Life* magazine assignment to write a piece on Joe and his wife Katie entitled "Ballplayer's Wife." Heinz knew that the pitcher was grasping for anything to ease the pain of declining abilities, and he promised to forget the piece. "I wished him luck and shook hands, and I left. End of story." In an effort to relieve Heinz's conscience, Lofting said that it was probably true that you couldn't write about losing in those days. "Only in literature," Heinz replied.

Heinz guessed, correctly, that he could raise Page's spirits by remi-niscing about his years as a Yankee. Thus, he spoke of some of the reliever's finest moments on the field, of teammates like DiMaggio and Berra, of managers Bucky Harris and Casey Stengel. While not dodging the subject of the young Page's reputation as a carouser, he did not dwell on it. He went out of his way to ask about visitors to the lodge who remembered Page and encouraged the ill man to speak of his love for his second wife and his sons. Upon leaving the Lodge, Heinz and Loft-ing were stopped by Mrs. Page. "I'm really pleased you two came," she said. "It's done a lot for him. It's been a long time since he's talked that much or sounded so well, or moved so well."

If Joe Page's loss was his fastball, Pete Reiser's was what might have been—and Heinz wrote his finest baseball piece about the former

Dodger. Reiser, he told Nathan Ward in 2004, was "my all-time guy. . . . When somebody risks his life the way he did, that to me is what professionalism is all about." In 1941, his first full year with the Dodgers, "Pistol Pete" led the National League in hitting (.343), runs (117), doubles (39), triples (17), and slugging (.558). He had lightning-fast speed—the Dodgers clocked him at 9.8 for 100 yards in his uniform and spikes. In 1946, he stole home seven times. Many believed that he was destined to be one of the game's superstars, perhaps its greatest "natural." "No doubt about it," Leo Durocher recalled, "he was the best I ever had, with the possible exception of Mays. At that, he was even faster than Willie."

Unfortunately, as Heinz pointed out in painful detail, Reiser's fearless and aggressive play ruined his career and almost cost him his life. In two and a half years in the minor leagues, three seasons of army ball, and 10 years in the majors, he was carried off the field 11 times. Seven times he crashed into the outfield wall. He was hitting .380 in 1942 when he ran full speed into a wall of concrete. Once, in 1946, the Dodgers clubhouse doctor called for a priest, who administered the church's last rites. He often played when he should have been in a hospital.

After his three years in the army (1943–1945), Reiser returned to the Dodgers, but he was never the same. The Dodgers gave up on him after the 1948 season, during which he hit only .236. He played two mediocre years with the Boston Braves (1949–1950), one with the Pirates (1951), and one with the Cleveland Indians (1952) of the American League. When Heinz caught up with him in the late 1950s, Reiser was managing the Kokomo (Indiana) Dodgers of the Class D Midwest League. He was only 39, but he walked "like an old man." "Did you ever think," Heinz asked him, "that if you hadn't played it as hard as you did, there's no telling how great you might have been?" Pete's answer was "never. If I hadn't played that way I wouldn't even have been whatever I was. God gave me those legs and the speed, and when they took me into the walls that's the way it had to be. I couldn't play any other way."

Heinz knew what Reiser's answer would be before he gave it because he understood what Roger Angell, another fine sports writer, observed years later: "Everyday baseball is stuffed with failure and defeat, overflowing with it, and for most of us who have followed the game over a distance, losing more and more appears to outweigh the other outcome as the years slip by, and at the same time deepens our appreciation of the pastime." That is so because *life* is primarily about losing: losing parents and other loved ones, friends, jobs, health, memory—life itself. Such losses are painful, but like losses in sports, they teach the valuable lesson of human limitation and shed light on the meaning of life. Heinz put it this way: "Everybody is a loser, let's face it. None of us wins every game, and none of us is going to live forever."

Heinz learned this as a war correspondent and made it explicit in a short story he wrote for the *Sun* in September 1949. Entitled "The Psychology of Horse Betting," it tells of two men discussing a psychiatrist's claim that people bet on horse races to lose, not to win. The more they think about it, the more convinced they become that the psychiatrist is on to something, something important. One of them says,

> There's the basic element of tragedy involved. The nearness of winning and then defeat is one thing all humanity understands. It's been the great force behind our literature, our art. The greatest books, the greatest plays have been tragedies. When they discuss the *Mona Lisa* they don't just talk about her smile. The great thing about it is the sadness of that smile. . . . There's something heroic about the ability to accept defeat. It's a role people accept, and enjoy more willingly than they know themselves.

They do so because that acceptance binds them to others by promoting mutual understanding.

The "basic element of tragedy involved" in the nearness of winning and then defeat is the subject of Heinz's most famous piece of writing—"Death of a Race Horse," published in the *Sun* on July 28, 1949. It recounts with memorable restraint the story of Air Lift, son of Bold Venture (winner of the 1936 Kentucky Derby and Preakness) and brother of Assault (winner of the Triple Crown in 1946). He was making the first start of what promised to be a great career. But after going into the turn, Air Lift slowed and then stopped; he had suffered a compound fracture of his left front ankle. After receiving word from the trainer and owner, the veterinarian destroys the unfortunate horse. It is impossible to *describe* the powerful effect Heinz's prose has had on readers. The following are his final few sentences:

They worked quickly, the two vets removing the broken bones as evidence for the insurance company, the crowd silently watching. Then the heavens opened, the rain pouring down, the lightning flashing, and they rushed for the cover of the stables, leaving alone on his side near the pile of bricks, the rain running off his hide, dead an hour and a quarter after his first start, Air Lift, son of Bold Venture, full brother of Assault.

In 1963, the same year *Run to Daylight!* appeared, Heinz published his second novel, *The Surgeon*. Like *The Professional*, it tells the story of a professional, in this case a thoracic surgeon. Heinz had come to know Dr. J. Maxwell Chamberlain, a distinguished thoracic surgeon who assumed life or death responsibilities on a daily basis. With Chamberlain's cooperation, he set out to write a reporter's account of the physician's work, but early in his research it became clear to him that "for this effort to obtain its objectives it would have to go beyond the beginnings and experiences of any one man." As a result, the book's 52-year-old Dr. Matthew Carter is a composite, and what began as a reportorial account became a novel.

Drawing upon Chamberlain's knowledge and experience, Heinz obtained an understanding of surgical practices so profound that he was able to describe actual cases (with the patients' names changed) in clinical detail. Then, as he had before, for example, in his account of Rocky Graziano's life on the day of a fight and Vince Lombardi's team preparation the week before an important game, he telescoped Dr. Carter's career into a single day, beginning with a wakeup call at 6:45 a.m. and ending with a difficult surgery at 2:55 p.m. Along the way, Heinz revealed personal experiences that made Dr. Carter not only the physician, but also the man he was. We learn that his parents were deeply religious but that having read Spinoza, Diderot, Holbach, Huxley, and Darwin in college, he lost what little faith he himself had.

But not for long. His experience of nature forces upon him a conviction that "there must be a God." In his first year of medical school, he witnessed an autopsy, and it dawned on him that "what they had removed would tell them why this now-manikin-man died, but it would not tell them why he had hoped and feared and lived." Having completed his studies and begun his practice, he would often tell others that, "[Y]ou can't witness the whole series of dynamic, immutable changes that is life from beginning to end without believing."

It was as a believing physician that Carter served in Europe during World War II. He operated for 24 hours straight in Normandy, all night in the kitchen of a church social hall in the Hürtgen Forest and all day during the Battle of the Bulge. There were surgical lessons to be learned, he concluded, from the choices officers made during battles—the surgeon had to make similar strategic choices as he approached the task before him.

Not all those on whom Dr. Carter operated during the war or, for that matter, during peacetime survived. "You have to learn to handle your deaths with grace," he would say. "You have to learn not to take them out on your associates, your wife, and certainly not on your next patient." That did not mean that you did not die a little with each person you lose—because you did. Losing, Carter—and Heinz—knows, is an inescapable part of life. You cannot pretend otherwise, nor can you allow it to paralyze you. In the novel, Carter loses Roberto Leon, a Brazilian suffering from cancer. A risky and difficult procedure alone could have saved him—and it failed.

Saving, or trying to save, the life of patients is not Dr. Carter's only responsibility. You soon learn, he says, "that for every patient you treat you've got to treat two or three or four relatives." In that regard, too, choices had to be made. Do you tell them the truth about the loved one's chances of survival, and if so, when? Some can handle the truth, but others cannot—at least not immediately. Some are relatively easy to deal with; others are difficult. Some treat you as a god, while others suspect you of incompetence. Dr. Carter is neither of course. He is a distinguished, but fallible, professional—and one, readers cannot be surprised to learn, who enjoys sports. He reads Red Smith's columns regularly and follows professional football, which also, he believes, holds lessons for surgeons. "Say you're a halfback going wide," he tells an intern. "You have to have two speeds. That's what we have. These chest openings are automatic, so we just go along one-two-three at top speed."

Dr. H. Richard Hornberger had studied under Dr. Chamberlain and sent him a letter in which he wrote that, "[T]hat clown who wrote your book might be interested that I have a book I put together from my experiences in Korea." Hornberger had served as a captain in the Army Medical Corps during the Korean War. His manuscript, entitled *MASH*, an acronym for mobile army surgical hospital, offered little in the way of a story line; it describes the hijinks of stressed-out doctors and other medical staffers, and surgeries performed in the most trying of circumstances. Because his wife Betty enjoyed reading the manuscript, Bill Heinz agreed to read and ultimately coauthor the book.

His first job was to clean up the text, "since it was full of those jokes that doctors like to make about the body." After that it was a matter of rewriting. *MASH: A Novel about Three Army Doctors* (1968) is held together by its memorable characters, especially three surgeons: Captain Benjamin Franklin Pierce, called Hawkeye (modeled after Hornberger); Captain Augustus Bedford Forrest, called Duke; and Captain John McIntyre, a thoracic specialist called Trapper. But there are others: long-suffering senior officer Lieutenant Colonel Henry Blake, Captain "Ugly" John Black, an anesthesiologist; Captain Walter Koskiusko Waldowski, a dental officer called the "Painless Pole"; Father Francis Mulcahy, called Dago Red; and Major Margaret Houlihan, chief nurse, called "Hot Lips" (by the men).

The doctors do a lot of drinking and generally raise as much hell as possible. Heinz may have been mildly amused, but he was primarily interested in Hornberger's accounts of the surgeries that Hawkeye, Duke, and Trapper John perform. There are times when they and those assisting them work anywhere from 12 to 16 hours a day, every day; sometimes they work 20 out of 24 hours trying to save the lives of badly wounded men. "Bellies, chests, necks, arteries, arms, legs, eyes, testicles, kidneys, spinal cords, all shot to hell. Win or lose. Life and death." One can imagine the pressure they were under. Heinz put it this way: "The business of doing major surgery on poor-risk patients can be trying and heartbreaking at any time, and when it is done regularly it can have an increasingly deleterious effect upon those who are doing it." This, of course, helps readers understand the surgeons' heavy drinking and irresponsible behavior when they have some time off.

Another reason for the physicians' seemingly inexplicable conduct is their inability to save everyone. We read, for example, of Angelo Riccio, a private from East Boston. A shell fragment hit his heart, causing hemorrhage in the pericardium, which surrounds and contains the heart—he was, in short, in serious condition. Trapper John sits down next to him and asks him how he thinks the Red Sox will do in 1952. The kid is not optimistic, because the "big guy" (Ted Williams) is himself somewhere in Korea. Williams, who served during World War II, reported for duty in Korea on May 1, 1952. As a marine captain, he flew 39 combat missions before returning to the Red Sox. Private Riccio would not be among the fans welcoming him back; despite Trapper and Duke's heroic efforts to save him, he dies.

Before *they* can return home, Hawkeye and Duke must help those who are due to replace them understand that their work at MASH is nothing like the work they did in the States. "Let me put it this way," Hawkeye says to one of the newcomers. "Our general attitude around here is that we want to play par surgery on this course. Par is a live patient. We're not sweet swingers, and if we've gotta kick it in with our knees to get a par that's how we do it."

After 18 months of duty, the army sends Hawkeye and Duke home to their awaiting families, but the two men know that their lives, like Heinz's life after the war, will never be the same. Never, except with their families, will they be as close to others as they were to those with whom they served—never, that is, will they again know such friendship. Others cannot possibly share their experiences. "I've been thinking," Hawkeye says to Duke as they are about to part ways, "that you and I really have been living a life that few of the people we're gonna meet from here on in know anything about."

MASH inspired a 1970 film directed by Robert Altman and written by Ring Lardner Jr. It won five Academy Award nominations and an Oscar for Best Adapted Screenplay. The film inspired a popular television series that ran from September 17, 1972, to February 28, 1983. Bill Heinz, however, had nothing to do with either the film or the series. He busied himself instead with *Emergency*, a novel he published in 1974. Another reflection on the medical profession, the novel revolves around people whose lives cross in a hospital emergency room. Some are members of the medical staff, while others are brought to the ER by fate.

Frank Baker has offered ambulance service to his community for more than 30 years, during which time he has come into contact with people from every walk of life. It is he who responds to a call to pick up a hit-and-run victim—Anita Wade, a nine-year old black girl. When he arrives at the scene, he finds detective sergeant George O'Donnell, a friend of many years. It was O'Donnell who, several years earlier, had been given the unhappy duty of telling Dr. Thomas R. Hunter, administrative head of the ER, that his teenage son had been killed when someone forced his car off the road into a bridge.

Dr. Hunter had served three years with the army in Europe during World War II. As a member of an armored medical battalion of an armored division, he had seen human beings at their best and worst. He tells a female reporter that he remembers that the "acts of sacrifice that men made again and again for the men beside them," but he also remembers the "horror of that slave-labor camp we liberated in our drive to meet the Russians on the Elbe." Even in the midst of the horror, however, he witnessed ill and starving prisoners crawl to a makeshift latrine rather than urinate or defecate among their fellows, and he knew again "that man is a noble creature."

Although Heinz does not identify it by name, the slave-labor camp was Dora-Mittelbau in the Harz Mountains. The prisoners were tasked with the excavation of underground tunnels that were to serve as the site of a plant for the manufacture of V-2 rockets. Those who were too sick or weak to perform labor were transferred to Nordhausen, a sub-camp, where they were starved to death. Dr. Hunter and his unit arrived after the U.S. Air Force had bombed a nearby airfield and, in the process, destroyed the camps. (In reality, the air force bombed the camps, believing them to be munitions depots.) "There were," he tells the reporter, "twenty-seven hundred dead of the bombing and of starvation and thirst and dysentery and tuberculosis and pneumonia, and hundreds more were to die every day."

The Americans, Dr. Hunter continues, forced local Germans to dig the "common graves, 60 feet long, 7 feet wide, and 4 feet deep, and we made them lay them side by side there."

> Then we bulldozed them over, and I remember a small boy of about eight, suddenly appearing, suddenly jumping into one of the long graves, the bulldozer positioning, hovering just above him. Who he was or what he was doing there I don't know, but he had recognized his father among all those almost look-alikes, and we had to pull him off, sobbing and screaming. What became of him after then I don't know.

But we, the readers, do know. The boy's name was Robert Ehrenberg. When he came of age, he changed his name to Bobby Carlton and began a modest career as a stand-up comedian. He happened to witness the hit-and-run and wanted to call the police, but as he tells his mother, "[I]t's tough in the business, and I'm lucky I'm even making a living. So

I call them and three months from now, or whenever it is, I'm a thousand miles from here and I get a subpoena and I blow a whole booking." Perhaps his conscience would have gotten the better of him, but before it could he suffers a massive and fatal heart attack, and expires in the ER.

There are no other known witnesses to the hit-and-run who can place Nicholas Braff, a jockey, at the scene of the crime, and he cannot bring himself to confess, although he makes repeated calls to the hospital in an effort to determine the girl's fate. In the end, his conscience will not let up, and he shoots himself in the head and dies in the ER. Some of the ER staff remember that he once was a well-known jockey, but they know little else. But they all know O'Donnell, who also arrives at the ER after having been shot while trying to arrest a petty criminal-turned-murderer. Every effort is made to save him, but the damage is too extensive. Dr. Hunter, who knew him well, tells his colleagues that he is again experiencing "that sensation of emptiness, that helpless, hollow feeling of frustration and nothingness that comes with that most total of all defeats, the sudden and intimate death." This is Heinz's way of saying, once again, that life is often about losing. He does not, however, leave readers without hope. On the last page of the novel, Anita Wade, the hit-and-run victim, shows signs of recovery.

Heinz's last original book was *Once They Heard the Cheers*. After 1979, he published collections of previously written pieces: *American Mirror* (1982), *What a Time It Was* (2001), and *When We Were One* (2002). In the foreword to *American Mirror*, Red Smith wrote that his "admiration for [Bill Heinz's] work is older than our friendship, which can be dated only with carbon 14." The feeling was mutual. In the "Author's Note" to the same book, Heinz wrote that he owed Smith "thanks not only for his words of introduction to this volume, but for a friendship that had grown to span 35 years."

During his last years, Bill Heinz cared for his wife Betty, who suffered from Alzheimer's disease. When she passed away in 2002, he moved to an assisted-living facility, where he died on February 27, 2008; he was 93.

5

AT TOOTS SHOR'S

In his memoirs, Granny Rice wrote, "Toots Shor is a friend of the world at large, barring all communists and hypocrites. In turn he is respected and loved by those that know him. A close friend of the athlete, sports writer, and columnist, Toots and 'Baby' his bride are tops in my little old book." When Granny died, Toots hosted a memorial party. Nothing could have been more fitting, because Granny and many of his friends, including Golden Age athletes and members of the fraternity of sports writers, were regulars at Shor's famous saloon and restaurant, located at 51 West 51st Street in Manhattan.

Bernard "Toots" Shor was born on May 6, 1903, in South Philadelphia. His parents, both of whom died tragically, were Orthodox Jews. When Toots was 15, his mother—who had given him his nickname—was killed by an out-of-control automobile while sitting on the front steps of her home; his father never recovered from his loss and, five years later, took his own life. Toots attended (briefly) the Drexel Institute of Technology and (for a year) the Wharton School of Business; for a time he worked for his cousin's Eclipse Shirt Company. But he was not cut out for the life of a businessman; there were, he concluded, more attractive opportunities awaiting him in New York. In 1930, he boarded a bus for Manhattan.

Having arrived on the island, he found work as a doorman and bouncer at such establishments as the Five O'Clock Club, the Napoleon Club, and Leon & Eddie's; for a time he ran Billy Lahiff's tavern. An imposing man with an even more imposing personality, Toots was like nothing so much as a character out of a Damon Runyon story. He liked to hang around gamblers, athletes, sports writers, gangsters, and show-girls, one of whom, Marian Volk, he married in 1934. Called "Baby" by everyone but Toots, who called her "Husky," the petite Mrs. Shor was a devout Catholic; the marriage was a happy one and resulted in four children.

Although outwardly gruff, Toots Shor had a soft heart and a gift for friendship (as did Rice, Smith, Povich, and Heinz). This, along with years of experience in the saloon and restaurant business, created in him an ambition to have a place of his own, and in 1940, he opened Toots Shor's. For the next 19 years, Shor's saloon/restaurant was *the* place for celebrities from all walks of life—and for those who wanted to rub elbows with them. The young Mickey Mantle was among the latter. "I used to sit at Shor's with Toots and Jackie Gleason, listening to Gleason tell stories. John Wayne came in all the time, and all the boxers came in, Rocky Marciano, Rocky Graziano, Billy Conn. I used to sit around and listen to their stories. God, I was 22 or 23 years old, and these guys were all like my heroes, and I'd just sit there and listen."

Toots mastered the art of the insult as a sign of friendship (his favorite word)—those whom he liked were "crumbums." It was, according to golfer Ken Venturi, "his term of endearment." To have Toots call you a crumbum meant that you were numbered among the favored. All the crumbums were, of course, men. Shor's was a place where guys were guys and women were dolls, dames, or broads. Women were ad-mitted, but only reluctantly. Men did not come seeking a pickup but hoping to meet friends. "We never looked at other women except our wives," Red Smith recalled. "This always interested Toots Shor. He used to crow about his 'special guys.' They didn't worry about dames."

As Toots told Patricia Lewis of the *Daily Express*, "[T]he people who made my place, the sports writers, the columnists, the guys like DiMag-gio and Joe Louis and Sinatra, they came there because it was a place they'd know their friends would be." They came too to drink. Shor's was, before anything else, a place to drink—to drink a lot. What food Toots offered was (very) basic American—steaks, potatoes, tomato soup. He would not allow anything on the menu that he could not pronounce or that required sauces.

Among Toots' less savory friends were Irish gangster Owney Mad-den (called, deservedly, "The Killer") and his more famous associate,

Italian mobster Frank Costello. At the same time, he welcomed to his place Francis Cardinal Spellman ("Spelly"), Chief Justice Earl Warren, and Mayor Jimmy Walker. He preferred, however, the company of athletes and sports writers. Among the former, in addition to boxers like Marciano and Graziano, were such football players as Frank Gifford and Charley Conerly (both of the New York Giants). Baseball players were, however, at the top of his list. At the top of that list was the "Yankee Clipper," Joe DiMaggio—until Toots made the mistake of saying something unflattering about Marilyn Monroe, to whom Joe was briefly, and famously, married. Other favored Yankees included Mantle, Billy Martin, and Whitey Ford. One can only surmise what Toots made of the cerebral Moe Berg, who often dropped in.

As we have seen, Grantland Rice was a regular at the establishment. And so was Red Smith. Red's son, journalist Terence Smith, recalls in his father's biography that Red "liked the attention he received, such as being given table number one—Toots had kind of a hierarchy of table placement—and he liked the fact that his son was watching all of this, all the famous people coming up to him." Just as important, Shor's place brought out Red's sense of humor. One evening he was cornered by Howard Cosell, who posed a question to him and other writers: "How many great sportscasters do you guys think there are?" Red replied, "One less than you think, Howard." At a dinner in Toots' honor just before he had to vacate 51 West 51st Street (he had sold his lease for $1,500,000), Red was one of the speakers. "When Toots turned 50," he said on that occasion, "we all gathered here to weep great, big, slobbery tears for a fat, drunken saloonkeeper. We're doing the same tonight."

Ten years later, Red wrote of a dinner held in honor of Toots' 40 years in New York; entitled "Crumbums," it was in a similar vein. "The price," he observed, "was $100 a head, which seems slightly ridiculous when you consider that celebrating 40 years of Toots Shor is like celebrating a broken hip. Actually, the crumbums came to salute themselves for survival." There were other comic lines, but Red grew serious (although not *deadly* serious) when he wrote of the kind of friend Toots was. A few hours after the Yankees swept the Phillies in the 1950 World Series, Toots was at his place when a waiter informed him that Joe Page had come to the bar. "The Fireman," we know, had a poor season in 1950, and played no role in the Series. In no mood to attend the team's victory party, he had left Yankee Stadium by himself. Toots jumped up from his table, and soon the waiter reported back: "The boss gave him a hero's welcome."

Like Granny and Red, Shirley Povich frequented Toots' place. In his autobiography, he recalled, "[W]e were virtually commuting to New York in the Forties and Fifties for all those good fights in the days of Joe Louis, Joe Walcott, Ezzard Charles, Gus Lesnevich, Archie Moore, Rocky Graziano, Tony Zale, Sugar Ray Robinson, Ike Williams, Kid Gavilan, Willie Pep, and Jake LaMotta." After a fight, he would head for Shor's. He was on his way there the evening of July 28, 1952, when he ran into Rocky Marciano, out for a stroll after knocking out Harry "Kid" Matthews in 2:04 of the second round in Yankee Stadium. Matthews had put up a game fight, but Marciano was the aggressor from the opening bell; two hard left hooks put his opponent down for the count. With that victory, Marciano earned a title shot at Jersey Joe Walcott.

Povich invited Rocky to accompany him to Shor's, where, to the amusement of everyone, the soon-to-be champion engaged Toots in a mock fight. In his autobiography, Povich pointed out that Toots took special pride in his ability to hold his own in confrontations with patrons. On one occasion, Povich recalled, he escorted a disorderly customer to the door with the words, "Outa my joint, ya bum!" The indignant ex-patron yelled, "You'll be sorry you did this, Shor. I'll never come back here with any of my business. Not only that, I'm going to tell all my friends." Toots replied, "Okay. Tell him."

In a similar spirit, Povich loved to needle Toots. One night, for example, he heard his friend praise a column by sports writer Bill Corum. "Who read it to you?" Shirley asked. Toots assumed the pose of Rodin's *The Thinker*. Someone at the table took Shirley to task, "You've hurt Toots' feelings." Toots quickly corrected him: "No he didn't. I was just trying to think who *did* read it to me."

There were, of course, more serious moments. One evening in the summer of 1954, Povich shared one of Toots' tables with jockey Eddie Arcaro, who spoke of the best sires of the day and his personal good fortune. "With his pretty wife Ruth," Povich wrote in the *Post*, "Arcaro is a figure on the Broadway scene. He dines out every night, makes most of the clubs, and is no teetotaler. Between riding engagements he is something of a bon vivant." And why not? In addition to riding fees that often hit $200,000 per year, he had oil-well interests, businesses in his native Kentucky, and part-ownership of a syndicate that staked 30 uranium claims in Utah and Colorado.

Like the other members of the fraternity, Bill Heinz enjoyed going to Toots' place, and he too sometimes met Arcaro there. On one occasion, when he was preparing his two-part essay on the great jockey, the two men lunched at Shor's and discussed riding tactics. "I was getting it from the master," Heinz wrote, "and that is the bonus of the business I am in." Even more important, Heinz knew that Ernest Hemingway frequented Toots' place, especially after fights—in fact, Toots would often accompany the famous writer to the Garden, or Yankee Stadium, or the Polo Grounds. "Anyone who hasn't known Toots," Hemingway once mused, "has missed something mighty important in life." The two men certainly had their share of booze (and then some) and laughs. Hemingway inscribed a copy of *Across the River and into the Trees* with "Dear Tootsie: Please ruffle the pages to let people think you read it."

Toots opened a new place at 33 West 52nd Street on December 27, 1961, but America was changing in ways that made it seem already a relic of the past. Never very good at the financial end of his business, Toots got himself into tax trouble; in 1971, the authorities closed his doors for nonpayment of federal, state, and local taxes in the amount of $269,516. Eighteen months later, he opened another restaurant at 5 East 54th Street, but the magic was gone. Moreover, Toots' health was deteriorating. He was in New York University Hospital in December 1976—with little time remaining to him. Red Smith did not wait for the end before writing a moving tribute, "World's Greatest Saloonkeeper," for the *New York Times*.

The opening paragraph was pure Red Smith.

> This is a holiday greeting to a friend who is spending Christmas in University Hospital, although he is not the university type. His name is Toots Shor. He is the greatest saloonkeeper in the world, and for more than 40 years he has been a major figure in sports in the Big Apple, friend and confessor and counsel to athletes, confidant of the sports hierarchy, fan, authority, raconteur. He ought to be designated a national landmark.

The place at 51 West 51st Street, Red continued, "was the mother lodge. Attendance was practically compulsory. If you wanted to see anybody, you went there." And if, Red wrote, the sought-after person happened not to be there, you could always settle for Hemingway, or Earl Warren, or Yogi Berra, or Billy Conn, or Frank Sinatra, or Jackie Gleason. "There never was a gathering place like it, and it seems improbable there will ever be another."

Toots Shor died on January 23, 1977, and there has never been another gathering place like the one in which he held court. Toots has become a symbol of a lost world, including the world of sports. One of the biggest losses, and not only for Toots and other New York baseball fans, was the relocation of the Dodgers and Giants to California after the 1957 season. After that, movement from one city to another became so common that it was not always easy to remember where a team was from year to year. Even more difficult was remembering where individual *players* were from year to year, the reserve clause having been successfully challenged legally.

The drug scourge has done even greater damage to the game. We know that many players from the 1940s and 1950s drank to excess, but drinking did not improve their play as "performance-enhancing drugs" do. From 1876 to 1994, the 50-home run mark was reached only 18 times; Hank Aaron, Frank Robinson, Reggie Jackson, Mike Schmidt, Ted Williams, Ernie Banks, and Eddie Mathews all failed to reach it. But from 1995 to 2002, the 50 mark was reached another 18 times, often by hitters who had never previously demonstrated much power. Luis Gonzalez, for example, had never hit more than 26 home runs in a season—until 2001, when he went on a rampage, belting 57.

The decline of boxing, according to Bill Heinz, was signaled by the closing, in 1961, of Stillman's Gym, located on Eighth Avenue between 54th and 55th Streets. The gym's proprietor was the tough, no-nonsense Lou Stillman (b. Lou Ingber), who once said that, "[B]ig or small, champ or bum, I treated them all the same—bad. If you treat them like humans, they'll eat you alive." Although he purposely kept his facility dirty and stiflingly hot, there came to it, Heinz wrote, "fighters from every continent but Antarctica, among them every heavyweight champion from Jack Dempsey through Floyd Patterson." No one, however, drew more onlookers than Rocky Graziano, which helps to explain why the gym plays a prominent role in the film *Somebody Up There Likes Me*.

For about five years, Heinz visited Stillman's at least once a week and "came to know philosophers who never heard of Plato, Aristotle,

Voltaire, or Kant, but found their own truths of life, and artists as dedicated to their own form of expression—boxing—as a man can be to any form." He attributed the fight game's decline to televised fights and greater opportunities for such underprivileged groups as black Americans. One might add, however, that there has been a notable absence of colorful fighters, the late Muhammed Ali being the exception that proves the rule.

There is something more, something that has come to infect all sports, with the notable exception of golf. Joseph Epstein, writer and sports fan, calls it "empty triumphalism." During the Golden Age,

> people saved strong congratulations for truly momentous victories: winning the final game of the World Series or the Stanley Cup, Wimbledon, and Olympic marathon run, the Kentucky Derby, and a few other select events. Now we have the touchdown dance, the sack dance, the Tarzan-of-the-apes scream after the slam dunk, the triple fist pump and knee raise after winning a mere point in tennis.

Still more important is the fact that sports are too much with us. Whereas, in the 1950s, there were 16 Major League Baseball teams, there are now 30. There are still only two leagues, the National and the American, but each is divided into three divisions—East, Central, and West. That means that six teams, not two, end the year in first place (in their divisions). So before we arrive at the World Series, we must first watch the Division Series (NLDS and ALDS) and the League Championship Series (NLCS and ALCS).

There are now 32 teams in the National Football League (NFL), 16 in the National Football Conference (NFC), and 16 in the American Football Conference (AFC). Each conference consists of four divisions (East, North, South, and West) made up of four teams. Before there can be a NFL championship game (Super Bowl), we must first have playoff series. The playoffs are made up of 12 teams, six from each conference: the four division winners and two "wild cards." So we have Wild Card Playoffs, Divisional Playoffs, and Conference Championships.

The National Basketball Association (NBA) numbers 30 teams, divided into two conferences of three divisions of five teams each. The top eight teams in each conference qualify for the playoffs, beginning with the Conference Quarterfinals (four matchups in each conference).

The four winners advance to the Conference Semifinals; the two winners then advance to the Conference Finals. The two survivors move on to the NBA Finals.

As we have seen, the National Hockey League (NHL) was, from the 1942–1943 season to the 1967–1968 season, comprised of six teams. It is now home to 30 teams, with the result that there must be three playoff rounds before the two surviving teams meet in the Stanley Cup Finals.

Then there are college sports: endless numbers of football games, capped by the College Football Playoff National Championship, and equally endless numbers of basketball games, capped by "March Madness," the National Collegiate Athletic Association (NCAA) Men's Division I Basketball Tournament. Coaches of these sports at big-time schools often make millions of dollars and are themselves the subjects of news reports and analyses. And of course the players themselves become national celebrities.

The vast number of these personalities and events would challenge the abilities of contemporary sports reporters—if they still had to report on all of them. But they do not, because fans can see them all on television or the Internet. In addition to NBC, ABC, and CBS, one can now tune in to ESPN, ESPN2, ESPN3, MLB TV, NBA TV, CBS Sports Network, the Golf Channel, the Tennis Channel, and the NFL Network. Football having replaced baseball as the "national pastime," gridiron fans can devote the better part of their lives to watching games, analyses, talk shows, specials, and documentaries.

The end of the Golden Age of Sports and the dominance of television coverage have brought an end to the golden age of sports writing. To be sure, there have been good writers since then—Jim Murray, Roger Angell, and Roger Kahn come to mind—but there has been no concentration of excellence to equal that made up by the members of the fraternity and colleagues such as Damon Runyon, Ring Lardner, John Lardner, Westbrook Pegler, Frank Graham, and Jimmy Cannon. Together these men elevated writing about sports to a level that has never been equaled and probably never will be.

BIBLIOGRAPHY

Alexander, Charles C. *Our Game: An American Baseball History*. New York: Henry Holt, 1991.

Allen, Frederick Lewis. *Only Yesterday: An Informal History of the 1920s*. New York: Harper Perennial Modern Classics, 2010 [1931].

———. *Since Yesterday: The 1930s in America, September 3, 1929–September 3, 1939*. New York: Harper & Row, 1972 [1939, 1940].

Angell, Roger. *Game Time: A Baseball Companion*, ed. Steve Kettmann. Orlando, FL: Harvest Books, 2003.

———. *Once More around the Park: A Baseball Reader*. New York: Ballantine, 1991.

Asinof, Eliot. *Eight Men Out: The Black Sox and the 1919 World Series*. New York: Henry Holt, 1987 [1963].

Beevor, Antony. *Ardennes 1944: Hitler's Last Gamble*. London: Viking, 2015.

Berkow, Ira. *Red: A Biography of Red Smith*. New York: Times Books, 1986.

Bohn, Michael K. *Heroes and Ballyhoo: How the Golden Age of the 1920s Transformed American Sports*. Washington, DC: Potomac Books, 2009.

Brown, Daniel James. *The Boys in the Boat: Nine Americans and Their Epic Quest for Gold at the 1936 Berlin Olympics*. New York: Penguin, 2014 [2013].

Christie, Matt. "On This Day: Muhammad Ali Toys with Poor Floyd Patterson." *Boxing News*, November 22, 2014.

Congdon, Lee. *Baseball and Memory: Winning, Losing, and the Remembrance of Things Past*. South Bend, IN: St. Augustine's Press, 2011.

———. "Nostalgia and Historical Memory." *World and I* 3, no. 8 (1988): 418–23.

———. "Ty Cobb." *Continuity* 11 (1987): 98–100.

Considine, Bob. *Toots*. New York: Meredith Press, 1969.

Dawidoff, Nicholas. *The Catcher Was a Spy: The Mysterious Life of Moe Berg*. New York: Pantheon, 1994.

Dodson, James. *Ben Hogan: An American Life*. New York: Broadway Books, 2005 [2004].

Epstein, Joseph. *Essays in Biography*. Mount Jackson, VA: Axios, 2012.

———. *Masters of the Games: Essays and Stories on Sport*. Lanham, MD: Rowman & Littlefield, 2015.

———. *Wind Sprints: Shorter Essays*. Edinburg, VA: Axios, 2016.

Farrell, James T. *My Baseball Diary*. Carbondale: Southern Illinois University Press, 1998 [1957].

Fitzgerald, F. Scott. *The Great Gatsby*. New York: Simon & Schuster, 1995 [1925].

Fountain, Charles. *Sportswriter: The Life and Times of Grantland Rice*. New York: Oxford University Press, 1993.

Frost, Mark. *The Grand Slam: Bobby Jones, America, and the Story of Golf*. New York: Hyperion, 2004.

Gittleman, Sol. *Reynolds, Raschi, and Lopat: New York's Big Three and the Yankee Dynasty of 1949–1953*. Jefferson, NC: McFarland, 2007.

Gray, J. Glenn. *The Warriors: Reflections on Men in Battle*. Lincoln: University of Nebraska Press, 1998 [1970].

Halberstam, David. *Summer of '49*. New York: William Morrow, 1989.

———, ed. *The Best American Sports Writing of the Century*. Boston: Houghton Mifflin, 1999.

Harper, William Arthur. *How You Played the Game: The Life of Grantland Rice*. Columbia: University of Missouri Press, 1999.

Heinz, W. C. *American Mirror*. Garden City, NY: Doubleday, 1982.

———. *Emergency*. Greenwich, CT: Fawcett, 1974.

———. *Once They Heard the Cheers*. Garden City, NY: Doubleday, 1979.

———. *The Professional*. Cambridge, MA: Da Capo, 2001 [1958].

———. *The Surgeon*. Garden City, NY: Doubleday, 1963.

———. *The Top of His Game: The Best Sportswriting of W. C. Heinz*, ed. Bill Littlefield. New York: Library of America, 2015.

———. *What a Time It Was: The Best of W. C. Heinz on Sports*. Cambridge, MA: Da Capo, 2001.

———. *When We Were One: Stories of World War II*. Cambridge, MA: Da Capo, 2002.

———, and Nathan Ward, eds. *The Book of Boxing*. Kingston, NY: Total Sports Illustrated Classics, 1999.

Hemingway, Ernest. *Across the River and into the Trees*. New York: Scribner, 2003 [1950].

———. *Hemingway at Oak Park High: The High School Writings of Ernest Hemingway, 1916–1917*, ed. Cynthia Maziarka and Donald Vogel Jr. Oak Park, IL: Oak Park and River Forest High School, 1993.

———. *Hemingway on War*, ed. Seán Hemingway. New York: Scribner, 2003.

———. *The Old Man and the Sea*. New York: Charles Scribner's Sons, 1953.

Hillenbrand, Laura. *Seabiscuit: An American Legend*. New York: Ballantine, 2001.

———. *Unbroken: A World War II Story of Survival, Resilience, and Redemption*. New York: Random House, 2014 [2010].

Holtzman, Jerome, ed. *No Cheering in the Press Box*, 2nd ed. New York: Henry Holt, 1995.

Hooker, Richard (Richard Hornberger and W. C. Heinz). *MASH: A Novel about Three Army Doctors*. New York: Harper Perennial, 2001 [1968].

Inabinett, Mark. *Grantland Rice and His Heroes: The Sportswriter as Mythmaker in the 1920s*. Knoxville: University of Tennessee Press, 1994.

Kahn, Roger. *The Era, 1947–1957: When the Yankees, the Giants, and the Dodgers Ruled the World*. Lincoln: University of Nebraska Press, 2002 [1993].

———. *A Flame of Pure Fire: Jack Dempsey and the Roaring '20s*. New York: Harcourt Brace, 1999.

Lardner, Ring. "The Battle of the Century." *GeorgesCarpentier.org*, http://georgescarpentier.org/the-battle-of-the-century-by-ring-lardner-1921 .

———. *Lardner on Baseball*, ed. Jeff Silverman. Guilford, CT: Lyons Press, 2002.

Large, David Clay. *Nazi Games: The Olympics of 1936*. New York: W. W. Norton, 2007.

Leavengood, Ted. *Clark Griffith: The Old Fox of Washington Baseball*. Jefferson, NC: McFarland, 2011.

Lombardi, Vince, with W. C. Heinz. *Run to Daylight! Vince Lombardi's Diary of One Week with the Green Bay Packers*. New York: Simon & Schuster Paperbacks, 2014 [1963].

Lytle, Andrew Nelson. *Bedford Forrest and His Critter Company*. Nashville, TN: J. S. Sanders, 1992 [1931].

MacSkimming, Roy. *Gordie: A Hockey Legend*. Vancouver, BC, Canada: Greystone Books, 2003.

Nathan, Daniel A. *Saying It's So: A Cultural History of the Black Sox Scandal*. Urbana: University of Illinois Press, 2005 [2003].

O'Toole, Andrew. *Strangers in the Bronx: DiMaggio, Mantle, and the Changing of the Yankee Guard*. Chicago: Triumph, 2015.

Povich, Shirley. *All These Mornings*. Englewood Clifts, NJ: Prentice Hall, 1969.

———. *All Those Mornings . . . at the Post: The Twentieth Century in Sports from Famed Washington Post Columnist Shirley Povich*, ed. Maury Lynn, David Povich, and George Solomon. New York: Public Affairs, 2005.

———. *The Washington Senators*. Kent, OH: Kent State University Press, 2010 [1954].

———. "The Year of '61." *Washington Post*, April 1, 1996, http://www.washingtonpost.com/wp-srv/sports/longterm/general/povich/maris.htm.

Rice, Grantland. *The Best of Grantland Rice*. Selected by Dave Camerer. New York: Franklin Watts, 1963.

———. *The Final Answer and Other Poems*. Selected by John Kieran. New York: A. S. Barnes, 1955.

———. *The Tumult and the Shouting: My Life in Sport*. New York: A. S. Barnes, 1954.

Roberts, Randy. *Joe Louis: Hard Times Man*. New Haven, CT: Yale University Press, 2010.

Ross, Ron. *Bummy Davis vs. Murder, Inc: The Rise and Fall of the Jewish Mafia and an Ill-Fated Prizefighter*. New York: St. Martin's, 2003.

Runyon, Damon. *Guys and Dolls and Other Writings*. New York: Penguin, 2008.

———. *Guys, Dolls, and Curveballs: Damon Runyon on Baseball*, ed. Jim Reisler. New York: Carroll & Graf, 2005.

Schaap, Jeremy. *Triumph: The Untold Story of Jesse Owens and Hitler's Olympics*. New York: Mariner, 2008.

Schulian, John. "How One of America's Greatest Sportswriters Disappeared." *Deadspin*, March 11, 2015, http://thestacks.deadspin.com/how-one-of-americas-greatest-sportswriters-disappeared-1690520123.

———. "W. C. Heinz Got to Heart of the Story." *Los Angeles Times*, March 1, 2008, http://articles.latimes.com/2008/mar/01/sports/sp-heinz1.

Shoemaker, Bill, and Barney Nagler. *Shoemaker*. New York: Doubleday, 1988.

Smith, Red. *American Pastimes: The Very Best of Red Smith*, ed. Daniel Okrent. New York: Library of America, 2013.

———. *Red Smith on Baseball*. Chicago: Ivan R. Dee, 2000.

———. *The Red Smith Reader*, ed. Dave Anderson. New York: Skyhorse, 2014 [1982].

———. *Sports Annual 1961*, ed. Verna Reamer. New York: Crown, 1960–1961.

———. *To Absent Friends from Red Smith*. New York: New American Library, 1982.

Socolow, Michael J. "Six Minutes in Berlin." *Slate.com*, July 23, 2012, http://www.slate.com/articles/sports/fivering_circus/2012/07/_1936_olympics_rowing_the_greatest_underdog_nazi_defeating_american_olympic_victory_you_ve_never_heard_of_.html.

Thomas, Henry W. *Walter Johnson: Baseball's Big Train*. Washington, DC: Phenom, 1995.

Turbach, Michael. *Saloonkeeper: Toots Shor in His Own Words and in the Words of Those Who Knew Him*. Curiosity, 2011.

Van Natta, Don, Jr. *Wonder Girl: The Magnificent Sporting Life of Babe Didrikson Zaharias*. New York: Back Bay Books, 2013 [2011].

Wallop, Douglass. *The Year the Yankees Lost the Pennant*. New York: W. W. Norton, 2004 [1954].

Walters, Guy. *Berlin Games: How Hitler Stole the Olympic Dream*. London: John Murray, 2006.

Ward, Nathan. "A Life in the Loser's Dressing Room." *American Heritage* 55, no. 4 (2004): 55–59. Interview with W. C. Heinz.

Watman, Max. "In the Ring Corner." *New Criterion* 24, no. 2 (October 2015): 77.

Wolfe, Thomas. *You Can't Go Home Again*. New York: Scribner, 2011 [1940].

DVDS

Chariots of Fire. On the 1924 Olympics.
Cinderella Man. The story of James J. Braddock.
Eight Men Out. Based on the book by Eliot Asinof.
Guys and Dolls. Based on stories by Damon Runyon.
Olympia. Classic film of the 1936 Berlin Olympic Games, produced and directed by Leni Riefenstahl.
Seabiscuit. Based on the book by Laura Hillenbrand.
Somebody Up There Likes Me. On the life of Rocky Graziano.
Toots: His Town. His Saloon.
Unbroken. Based on the book by Laura Hillenbrand.

YOUTUBE

1952 WS Gm 7: Martin Makes Running Grab in Infield
Berlin 1936 Rowing Eight
Billy Graham W 10 Carmen Basilio I
Boxer Dies in Ring: Benny "Kid" Paret and Emile Griffith
Fildeo de sandy Amoros Serie Mundial 1955
Gene Tunney vs. Jack Dempsey/1926 World Heavyweight Championship
The Greatest Homerun Ever: Bill Mazeroski 1960 Walk-off Home Run
Ingemar Johansson vs. Floyd Patterson I
Ingemar Johansson vs. Floyd Patterson II
Jack Dempsey and Jess Willard—the Worst Beating in Boxing History
Jack Dempsey vs. Gene Tunney—the Long Count (1927)
Jack Dempsey vs. Georges Carpentier (July 2, 1921)
Jack Dempsey vs. Jack Sharkey (July 21, 1927)
Jack Dempsey vs. Luis Angel Firpo (Sept. 1923)
Joe Louis vs. Billy Conn (I)
Joe Louis vs. Billy Conn, II
Joe Louis vs. Ezzard Charles
Joe Louis vs. James Braddock Highlights HD
Joe Louis vs. Jersey Joe Walcott, I
Joe Louis vs. Jersey Joe Walcott II
Joe Louis vs. Max Schmeling I and II (Highlights)
Joe Louis vs. Max Schmeling, II (Full Film, HD)
Joe Louis vs. Primo Carnera Rounds 5 and 6
Joe Louis vs. Rocky Marciano
Joe Louis vs. Tami Mauriello
Kid Gavilan vs. Billy Graham III 29.8.1951 (Selected Round Highlights)
Max Baer vs. Joe Louis—All Rounds
Muhammad Ali Punishing Floyd Patterson and Being Cruel
Muhammad Ali vs. Floyd Patterson II 20.9.1972 (Selected Round Highlights)
Muhammad Ali vs. Floyd Patterson HD
Randy Turpin vs. Sugar Ray Robinson I
Rocky Marciano vs. Archie Moore (All Rounds)
Rocky Marciano vs. Harry "Kid" Matthews in 1952
Rocky Marciano vs. Jersey Joe Walcott, I
Rocky Marciano vs. Jersey Joe Walcott II—May 13, 1953
Rowing—Summer Olympics—Berlin 1936
Seabiscuit vs. War Admiral—1938 Match Race (Pimlico Special)
Seabiscuit Wins the 1940 Santa Anita Handicap

Sugar Ray Robinson vs. Carmen Basilio (I)
Sugar Ray Robinson vs. Carmen Basilio II 1958 03 25
Sugar Ray Robinson vs. Randy Turpin II
Tony Zale vs. Rocky Graziano III

INDEX

ABOUT THE AUTHOR

Lee Congdon is professor emeritus of history at James Madison University. He is author of *Baseball and Memory: Winning, Losing, and the Remembrance of Things Past*; *George Kennan: A Writing Life*; and three other books. Congdon has been a Fulbright research scholar in Budapest and a visiting member of the Institute for Advanced Study at Princeton.